I Sneezed in My Casket!

I Sneezed in My Casket!

For God Cannot Lie

Joel R. Jeune, D.D.

as told to
Bob Armstrong
and
written by
Marlon Migala

Library of Congress Control Number: 2009905252
ISBN: Hardcover 978-1-4415-4122-2
Softcover 978-1-4415-4121-5

Unless otherwise indicated, all scriptural quotations are taken from the King James Version of the Bible.

This book was printed in the United States of America.

To order additional copies of this book, contact:
Grace International
1-305-231-1117
www.graceintl.org
office@graceintl.org

57069

CONTENTS

DEDICATION

I dedicate this book to the glory of the Almighty God.

Without my precious lifelong helpmate, my wife Doris, I could not have accomplished as much for the Lord and our Haitian people. My life and ministry remains vital and strong because of her love, support and strong work ethic. How can I thank her enough?

I especially thank my four sons who have probably suffered very much because of the ministry burden that Jesus has bestowed upon me.

To my brother Amos Jeune and sister Marthe who have been such a great help and support to us from the very beginning of this ministry.

To Jonny, Joel, Danny, Michael, our adopted daughter Joanne Jeune and all our non biological sons and daughters who have been raised in our children's homes we say a big thank you for your support and wish that you will always greatly succeed in everything you do for Him.

My grateful appreciation to the Gerald Derstine Family who sponsored my wife through her childhood.

To the precious Helman family: Leslie, Dick, Joyce and Vanis, for contributing to my wife's education and my son's college.

To Dr. Luke Weaver: for encouraging me to share my testimony with the world and helping me to do so for the first time on the 700 Club. Thanks for prayerful, emotional and nonstop financial support for more than 37 years.

To Pastor Billy Joe and Sharon Daugherty: for giving my dad and I the opportunity to be on Richard Roberts show to share this testimony with its television audience.

To Paul and Jan Crouch for allowing me the opportunity on TBN to tell their viewers about the resurrection power of God.

I am eternally grateful to my dad, Bishop Rameau D. Jeune for his great faith in God's promise which resurrected me from the dead and lifelong gratitude to my mother who taught me God's Word and how to live right. I am very thankful to my biological brothers and my sister for their support as I was growing up. I am also very appreciative of the many leaders and pastors I've had the privilege of working alongside through the struggles and victorious years.

I cannot thank enough my many friends, prayer and financial partners who have helped to make the lives of so many, much better. I would like to thank my friend, Rev. Bob Armstrong, for his assistance in tape recording and transcribing the verbal account of my life. I have seen, first hand, his heart for the Haitian people.

I would also like to thank my friends Marlon and Jerri Migala for their encouragement and assistance in making this dream a reality. Thanks to Marlon for his dedication in writing, editing and indexing my vocally expressed biography and for writing this book into the highly readable result that I trust you will enjoy and be inspired by. I Thank God, from whom all our blessings flow!

FOREWORD

I have personally known Joel Jeune for most of the years of his life. I gave him permission to marry the girl who is now his wife and mother of all his children. Joel has always lived a life of Biblical diligence and holiness and set an example of Godliness and leadership to the multitudes of his Haitian counterparts as pastors and ministers in Haiti.

Joel has been diligent in fulfilling his Call as a Christian leader, and has faithfully mentored many young men to become pastors, evangelists and teachers of the Word of God, the Holy Bible. My wife Beulah and I have accepted Joel and his wife Doris as a part of our family and enjoyed observing their Christian development in the nation of Haiti.

I can say their lives have been an inspiration to untold thousands of people world-wide. This book will be an inspiration to the many who read its incredible story which truly was a miracle of God.

Dr. Gerald G. Derstine
Chairman of the Board,
Gospel Crusade, Inc.
Gospel Crusade Ministerial Fellowship, Founder-Chairman,
President, Strawberry Lake Christian Retreat Church, Inc.
Founder, Director of Israel Affairs, International

Dr. Phil and Dr. Gerald Derstine with Dr. Joel Jeune at his doctorate graduation ceremony

PREFACE

Joel Jeune is a man of God. He has proven himself over the years. Sharon and I have ministered in Port au Prince on several occasions in the past twenty years. We had the joy of talking with his father and hearing the spirit of faith in this man. Joel and Doris have given their lives to minister the love of Jesus to the people of Haiti. The fruit of churches across the nation and thousands of children trained in their schools is evidence of their labor of love. We also had the joy of Danny Jeune attending Victory Christian School in Tulsa for a period of time. He exemplified the character of Jesus that was in his parents. You will be thrilled reading the story of Joel's life and inspired by the miracles he has experienced in walking out God's plan for his life. Being in their home and watching them live for Jesus has given me the confidence to say these people are authentic Christians.

Dr. Billy Joe Daugherty
Pastor, Victory Christian Center
Tulsa, Oklahoma

PRELUDE

The ministry of Bishop Joel Jeune is not new to the Osborn Family. From our first introduction to him nearly three decades ago, we have remained friends of his growing ministry. As a young man the call of God was evident in his life.

The Osborn Ministries International invested many "Tools for Evangelism" into Bishop Joel's ministry, confident that he was passionate about helping people through the power of Christ and His Gospel. Today Bishop Joel and his wife Doris are leaders of a pacesetting ministry that is doing the work of Christ in a hurting world. We salute their lives as extensions of the life of Christ on the earth, and consider it an honor to call him our "friend in the Gospel."

Bishop LaDonna Osborn
Osborn Ministries

INTRODUCTION

Faith to Overcome-Economic Upheaval

My heart is constantly full of joy and my eyes filled with tears for the people of Haiti, a people who are strong, resilient and beautiful even in the worst of circumstances. The nation of Haiti has the poorest economy in the western hemisphere but much worse is its "spiritual condition." Haiti has instilled, in me, much meaning for my life; as I believe God has called me to create change and transformation for my people. Haiti was once a thriving producer of multiple exports and a greatly desired leisure destination; now there is little production or a vacation industry to speak of because the social and physical environment has been fractured and all but destroyed. A history of political corruption and instability has repeatedly sparked violence and unrest, resulting in a barrage of negative press internationally. This heavy reality has resulted in the long demise of Haiti's tourism industry; many companies leaving due to the social chaos and governmental turmoil. In all honesty, Haiti has existed in a very unfavorable situation for decades. Actually, many of us have struggled and prayed for democratic elections for decades; we the people choosing our own freely elected representatives. Our hopes and dreams are slowly coming to pass.

Thank God for a new day dawning in Haiti! The people are gaining confidence to speak up for change, for peace and for a renewed country! Much of this transformation is happening as the "spiritual condition" is being changed. Churches and organizations across the country are banding their members together to pray, to learn, to be equipped and to speak up; to take responsibility for our beautiful island in every way possible. I am sure you have heard the horror stories about Haiti, yourself, many of which are true. Now, I would like you to hear a different story, one with a different perspective; a view where hope prevails and God keeps His promises. My prayer for you, as you read my story, is that you will laugh, cry and try to comprehend all the miracles that God has provided; that you will be challenged to have peace and victory in your life. I pray that you will stand on God's promise and proclaim, as my dad once did, that God cannot lie. I speak resurrection to every dream, every marriage, every business, and every vision that's in a casket on the way to the cemetery. I speak life in Jesus' Name!

"Then the word of the Lord came unto me, saying, before I formed thee in the belly, I knew thee. Before thou comest out of the womb, I sanctified thee and I ordained thee a prophet unto the nations. Then said I, Lord God, behold, I cannot speak for I am a child, but the Lord said unto me, say not I am a child, for thou shalt go to all that I shall send thee and whatsoever I command thee, thou shalt speak. Be not afraid of their faces, for I am with thee to deliver thee, sayest the Lord. Then the Lord put forth His hand and touched my mouth. And the Lord said unto me, Behold, I have put My words in thy mouth. See, I have this day, set thee over the nations and over kingdoms, to root out and to pull down and destroy, to build and to plant." Jeremiah 1:4-10

SPIRITUAL VICTORY IN HAITI

By Marlon Migala

Everyone loves to read a great adventure story; all the more so if it's truth not fiction. The brave men and women, who scaled the Mount Everest's of the world, flew the first transoceanic crossings; landed on the moon or rescued those imperiled by disasters or calamities all inspire us with their heroic exploits.

This spiritual journey, which you are about to read, is replete with the miracles that attended a man born of humble circumstances who, with inspiration from an even more challenged father, found God and allowed his spirit to be transformed by the presence of Christ whom he invited to be his savior.

His destiny was prophesied, by God, to a father whose own life had been transformed from poverty and violence to salvation and purpose.

At two years old, he fell ill and died only to be resurrected when his father challenged God about the truth of His prophetic promise. Through one trial and tribulation after another, as might be expected of a Haitian boy growing up Christian, he prevailed in a country bedeviled by Voodoo.

Joel Jeune's steadfast resistance in the face of obstacles, of all magnitudes, earned him a following and reputation befitting a man of God.

When the battle lines, with the devil and his Voodoo converts, were drawn at Bois-Caiman; the man of God drew thousands of supporters both in Haiti and around the world.

Life threatened, thrown into jail, vexed by Voodoo magic tricks; Pastor Joel, now Bishop over a multitude of churches and God's people, soldiered on. The Haitian government, of that time, sent gangs of thugs to disrupt and destroy the anti Voodoo rally at Bois-Caiman. Amazingly God set ablaze the Voodoo Tree, sending its worshippers fearfully fleeing into hiding or a resultant death.

After January 12, 2010; perhaps the greatest challenge faced Bishop Joel, Pastor Doris and Grace International's nearly four decades long ministry. Approximately 25,000 survivors of a 7.2 level seismic earthquake sought refuge at Grace Village within the sheltering confines of the Lamentin and Waney campuses.

Many years ago, Bishop found 15 girls, orphaned, homeless and adrift in a 'Sea of Sorrows' spawned by a devastating hurricane named Alicia. Bishop rescued and brought the girls home with him. Pastor Doris was presented with the first residents of her, wished for, orphanage.

From this modest beginning the Jeunes were now sheltering thousands ('Orphans of the Storm') displaced from home and hearth by a cataclysm of unprecedented magnitude that killed hundreds of thousands and left more than a million homeless.

Jesus parable of the "Good Samaritan" is one of the cornerstones of His Prophetic Christianity, teaching us and showing us the Way we should live our lives and travel the Road before us. So also, by their own example, Bishop Joel and Pastor Doris Jeune have shown us how to imitate Christ in our own walks of life.

By opening the gates of Grace Village and welcoming thousands of devastated, displaced and disheartened fellow Haitians out of their 'Sea of Sorrows' into the 'Safe Harbor' of Gods 'Sheltering Safe Space' they are truly Good Samaritans.

Where there was but a village, a town of tents and tarps soon sprung up; offering hope where there was helplessness, health where disease might have been rampant and food where hunger hovered. The Lords Kitchen program fed hundreds unto thousands.

Empowerment to the embattled is underway! God's word is being broadcast, by Grace's pastors circulating among the new residents of this Oasis of Faith as well as over a P.A. system announcing the Good News through praise music and Bishops encouragements and biblical readings.

The immediate, post earthquake, challenges encountered daily by the survivors were, obtaining safe potable water and sufficient food. Initially, Grace Village; having been surveyed by the U.N., the U.S. Navy, Marines and governmental representatives and found to be a peaceful and well organized enclave; became the designated distribution center for humanitarian supplies (food, good water etc.) for a large segment of the city of Carrefour. Along with the thousands who had hunkered down on Grace's campus grounds, some 100,000, during the course of each week, came to seek sustenance and relief.

Doctors With Out Borders, whose own facilities had been destroyed and compromised out of useful commission, moved into Grace's hospital at our compound. Under the stewardship of Jonny Jeune (himself a licensed general contractor) our hospital (originally intended to serve children and mothers) built to strict California earthquake resistance standards, became a general hospital.

With most of the other hospitals and medical facilities, in the greater Port Au Prince/Carrefour area, either destroyed or rendered dysfunctional, thousands came for treatment. Doctors With Out Borders, employing dozens of Haitian physicians and nurses ministered there to hundreds of patients each day.

Though limbs were lost, lives were saved. Diseases spawned by devastation were defeated. The road of destruction was transformed into a highway of hope for tens of thousands with nothing left to lose.

The road to normalcy may be long but Haitians are strong. They are a people, historically born of hope, who have survived enslavement, exploitation, dictators and degradation.

Their land once known as "The Pearl of the Antilles", can, with a little help from its friends, once more become a garden of grace, a beacon of beauty; shining out to the world as a model of miracles, a success story written with the creativity and toiling steadfast sweat of its resilient people and the word of God manifested by His grace.

CHAPTER 1

In The Beginning

My great grandparents came from a family who were strong worshippers of the Voodoo religion. We also came from a presidential family, because one of my great grandparents, Lucius Solomon Jeune, was the president of the Republic of Haiti. Although I have a president in my bloodline, I came from a pastoral family originating in a little town named Morency-Cayes. My dad, brothers, uncles, cousins, nephews, etc., have been and some 39 in my family line are now pastors serving the Lord. I thank God for that.

My grandfather on my father's side was a Voodoo man whose lively hood, during the pre-Castro years, was fishing and transporting people from Haiti to Cuba to cut sugar cane. Rameau Jeune, my father, assisted grandpa in fishing and ferrying workers to Cuba. My father, then a young man of about 15 to 18 years old, decided to stay in Cuba to cut sugarcane and work other jobs. There was more money cutting sugarcane than what he was earning working with his father.

My father lived in Cuba for 17 years and cohabited with a lady named Camela Louissaint by whom, though they were not legally married, he had three boys: San Juan Jeune, Ferdinand Jeune, and Leonard Jeune.

In those years my dad was a very mean man who was not saved and did not know the Lord. He fought a lot because of his bad temper and got into many arguments. His bad temper, didn't allow anyone to witness the Lord to him. He cursed at and beat up anyone who tried to preach the Gospel to him.

DAD SAW THE LIGHT

One day, two missionaries came to preach to Dad and tell him all about Jesus. He beat them up, punching their faces and shouting, "I am my own God!"; proclaiming that he was God, himself. He refused to permit anyone to tell him that he was bad or that he needed God and the missionaries told him, "We don't give you long before you become a Christian! This God we are telling you about; you'll get to know Him one way or another."

Two weeks after that encounter, my dad got involved in a big fight with six, machete wielding, men. My dad killed two of the men in that terrible melee and ran away, from the police, to hide in the sugarcane field. Unknown to dad, who was hiding and surviving on sugar cane in that field, there was a little church right behind it. That little church had services three times a week so, while hiding for 15 days, he was constantly hearing the Gospel and listening to the singing, the preaching and the prayers.

One day as the pastor was preaching from Isaiah chapter one, he quoted the verse that says, "If your sins are as crimson, the Lord will make it as white as snow." The preacher insisted, "If you are a criminal, if you shed the blood of people, don't try to hide from God for He sees where you are hiding and you cannot run away from Him. Come out and give your heart to the Lord and He will forgive you, wash away your sins and set you free!"

Upon hearing what the pastor so strongly proclaimed, dad thought that someone had seen him hiding there, so he just ran out of the cane field into the church and gave his heart to the Lord. He cried out asking God to transform his life and to forgive him for all his sins, all his pride and for the men that he had killed. They prayed for him and he accepted Christ in his heart. He was gloriously saved!

Dad confessed to the pastor who he was, what he was doing there and where he came from. A few days later, the pastor encouraged him to go to the police and the judge, to make it right. At first dad didn't want to do this but finally decided to go, with the pastor, and explain what had happened to the police and the judge. They detained him for a few days while calling in some of the other men who were involved in the fight. After the judgment, he was set free because it turned out to be self-defense: six men against one.

After being released from jail; Dad served the Lord, at a church in Cuba, for about three to six months. After being baptized in water, the Lord spoke to his heart telling him not to keep this good news to himself but to go back home to Haiti bringing the good news of the Gospel and the new life he had received. Thus, he left his children with their mother and moved back to Haiti to share this profound change in his life with his family who were devoutly serving Voodoo.

He told them about this life changing time he had experienced with Christ. At that time, immersed as they were in Voodoo, they knew nothing about the Gospel. They missed him so much during the 17 years he was away that they immediately accepted him back home as a member of the family but they rejected his message and his new religion. Some of them secretly plotted an attempt to kill him.

THEY TRIED TO POISON MY DAD

A few of his own people started putting poison, in his water, food and drinks but they were surprised and chagrined that their poison was not killing him. Thinking that maybe their poison wasn't strong enough; they increased the dosage and tried it out on the dogs and cats who promptly died and then tried it on him again. They gave him three times the original amount because in Voodoo they believed in the number three, which was supposed to have power to do their bidding. That didn't work so they tried seven times the dose of poison because they believed that seven was an even stronger number that held more power to accomplish their deed but that was not successful, either. They were determined to kill Dad and tried 14 times the dosage of poison but to no avail. Still alive, he continued preaching to them. Twenty one times they poisoned his food trying to kill him but the power of God saved his life despite all those despicable attempts to murder him.

Finally, they gave up trying to kill Dad instead asking him some intelligent questions, "Rameau, tell us about poison in your religion?" He told them that the Bible says, if you are Christian and believe in Jesus; this is one of the signs that will follow those who believe. Mark 16 says, "In my name, they shall drink any deadly thing and it shall not hurt them. They shall lay hands on the sick and the sick shall recover. They shall cast out demons and they shall speak in new tongues." They confessed that they did not like what he was preaching but since he was family, they could not reject him publicly or openly; instead trying to poison him to death.

They exclaimed, "We have tried as many as 21 times to poison you, but you are still alive! We want the religion that you are preaching to us because it is so powerful it can keep us from dying from poison!"

My grandmother, all my father's brothers, his sister, my uncles aunts; all repented and gave their hearts to Jesus. My Dad started his first church at home with his own family. A few weeks later, many of his cousins, neighbors and others; upon hearing this astounding witness, gave their hearts to the Lord in that first little home church.

My dad discipled Beauvil and Levy Jeune, two of his younger brothers, who had expressed great interest in the Gospel; whereupon they also started preaching and ministering in this new family church. Later, these brothers left to attend a small Baptist Bible School; which later became the great MEBSH Haiti South Baptist Mission.

After my dad established that little home church in his family's village of Morency-Cayes in Haiti, he returned to Cuba; attempting to bring Camela and their three boys back to Haiti with him to her home town of St. Louis, du Sud. They were, however, incompatible. Perhaps she didn't want to accept Christ as her Savior or to get married. A few years after they returned to Haiti they separated, never having married.

Their three sons St. John, Ferdinand and Leonard went on to become Christian leaders and pastors. Leonard went on to become National Superintendent/Bishop of the Pentecostal Church of God of Haiti.

DAD PREACHING ON THE MOUNTAIN

Dad left St.Louis du Sud, migrating westward to the capital of Haiti, Port-au-Prince. Afterward he traveled east to Fonds-Parisiens, Fonds-Verrettes and Forêt-des-pins; where I was born. On the way, he continued preaching, telling people about Jesus. However, he was confronted with many trials as he traversed the unpaved roads. Dad worked, for 20 cents a day, helping to build a dirt road up to Forêt-des-pins, to sustain himself and to support his preaching. Some other preachers that he encountered along the way were so jealously angry at him that they used their local influence to get Dad thrown into jail in Fonds-Parisiens.

After being released he continued traveling eastward and met my mother's family while preaching the Gospel in her village of Fonds-Verrettes. He was opposed by both Voodooists and Catholics as well as Baptists who disagreed with his exposition about the Holy Ghost. This evangelism resulted in his being jailed several times.

My mother's parents were Frère Jean and Madame Jean Casséus. They and my mother accepted Christ as a result of Dad's preaching. Shortly afterward my father and mother became engaged and Dad continued to preach, evangelize and disciple Christian converts in and around Fonds-Verrettes for several years after which they were married.

My mother's first born boy was Amos Jeune and two years after that she birthed me. My father was Bishop Rameau Dantès Jeune and my mother was Martine Casseus. Both are now deceased.

The Church at Canaan Thiotte, one of 35 churches dad founded

Feeding the school children in the mountains

CHAPTER 2

Stop The Funeral

"Aahchew!"

A child's sneeze was heard emanating from within the little coffin.

I was born on a little mountain in Eastern Haiti, in a village called Petite-Source at Foret-des-pins, Fonds-Verrettes County near the border of the Dominican Republic. My father was Bishop Rameau Dantes Jeune and my mother was Martine Casseus. Both are now deceased.

Five days prior to my birth, while awaiting an expected daughter, my dad received a Holy Ghost prophecy that he would be blessed by a son.

"This baby is going to be a boy. He is going to grow up to be a minister. He is going to preach and do a great work on the island of Haiti."

During the first two years of my life, my dad continued preaching in the mountains; traveling to other villages, establishing out stations and churches but he was not allowed to preach in his home village.

At two years old, I got very sick with dysentery. Since there were no medical services in our village, then or now, no one really knew what was ailing me. My symptoms were diarrhea and vomiting. My little body became very dry and dehydrated. Dad, who was on a preaching trip, came home and prayed for me. He left again because he had an appointment with a group of young Christians to go to another village and there to establish a church. He believed that God was going to heal me because of the prophetic promise, from God, on my life.

Keeping his appointment, he met with the others and traveled on his mission from village to village walking ever farther and many hours away from home.

While my father was away the unexpected happened. My family, the midwife and other concerned friends and villagers called the authorities who confirmed that I died. Little baby Joel had passed away. Village people came in and cried in the room where my body lay. There was no morgue, funeral home or any other place for a dead body. The room where the death occurred was cleared and mourners gathered there.

A messenger was dispatched the day I died to find my dad and tell him to return home because there was a death in the family. My dad had moved on from where he was thought to be so he was not found that day.

Two days later, my dad, still not having returned; my mother decided, to go ahead with the funeral because my dead body was starting to decompose. They made up a little coffin; my casket! Everything was ready. The Christians who were there prayed and held the wake in our home. People mourned and cried, even on their way to the local cemetery, about 3 miles away.

The funeral procession had already traveled two and one-half miles; when my dad, who had finally been informed of my death, met the procession going to the cemetery, with the little casket. Dad said, "What is going on?" They said, "Well, little Joel surely died and the body was decomposing, so we could not wait for you. We had to go on to the cemetery and bury him." My dad commanded, "Put the coffin down! I know that God cannot lie to me. My son cannot die!" So they put the little casket down and he said to them, "This is what God told me, before Joel was born. God told me he was going to be a boy and that he was going to grow up to do a great work for the island of Haiti. I know that God cannot lie, so put him down. Let us believe God for a miracle!"

There were a few Christians among the mourners and they prayed with my father for one and a half hours. Some in the group believed not in prayer but in Voodoo. All were waiting to see what would happen. The little casket remained unopened.

An hour passed with no change and the little box remained still and motionless, all were quietly waiting on the Lord.

My praying Dad called out to God, saying, "Lord, if You want me to continue to serve You, then You must give me this miracle! You can't deny me before all these people that do not know Jesus; that believe in Voodoo. You have to do a miracle, if You want me to continue serving You!"

After another hour and one-half in the heat of Haiti, the non believers among the people were insisting, "Let's go on to the cemetery." Suddenly, something happened! They heard a child sneeze!

Everybody was surprised, because they knew that children were not allowed to follow a funeral procession, especially one for a little child. They looked around and saw no other children. Somebody thought the sneeze was coming from in the casket but all refrained from doing something until they were sure that the sound was not coming from another child in the crowd.

They decided to open the little casket. When dad saw that my body was moving and that I was breathing ever so slightly he realized that God had restored life into my small, dead body! Dad pulled me out of that little casket and holding me carefully in his arms, for I was very sick and weak, carried me back home. He told me later that, on our way home, I had started calling, "Papa, Papa, Papa." That day, the funeral was cancelled!

Now I can see that the devil was rejoicing when I was dead, en route to the cemetery; happy that they were going to bury me. The dream and the promise that my dad had received would be no more, because the devil was going to bury God's prophecy. Some were saying, "God is a liar, He said, Joel Jeune was going to do a great work on the island, now he is on his way to the cemetery. We are going to bury him."

Praise God, it is never too late for Him. God always keeps His promises. When times look dark and impossible, for man, God can make a miracle. We are so thankful that God is the God of resurrection.

Everyone there, including those that did not believe were surprised by the miracle of my resurrection and started praising God; even though they did not know what to say. "We never saw anything like that before! We did not know that prayer could do that!" Escorting my dad and me on the way home some of them stopped at the police station and told the police chief what had happened.

My father had been arrested and jailed five times previously for preaching the new religion, so different from Voodoo, in his village. They had, on those occasions, told the chief of police, "If this man is arrested and jailed again, we will all go to jail with him because we want the power that he is preaching about. We want this new religion that he has come to give us." That having been said, the chief set dad free and he was allowed to preach in the village where he established its first church.

God moved that mountain so His word would be established in that village. What miracle you are waiting for? Will God receive glory through your miracle?

In a few weeks I was healed and started getting my strength back. Today, in my adulthood, I understand what God was doing and I am reminded by my elders of the miracle of my resurrection so many years ago.

I remember many people coming to my dad's home; some from so far away that they could not return home the same day. People always wanted to see me but not my siblings and I didn't know why. I never understood until they told me about the resurrection miracle. It was because of this miracle that people came to see for themselves the boy who had been redeemed from death and that was a stimulant to their faith to receive their own miracles.

When I was four years old another miracle happened. My mother, six year old brother and I embarked on a four-hour trip astride a horse. In the middle of the trip my hands got very tired of holding on to the saddle and got loose. I fell off the horse, splitting my head nearly in half against a rock in the road. My Mother grabbed me and tied my bleeding head with a towel. She had no first aid kit or any medicines to treat me with and we had to travel almost an hour before finding a house where she got some salty water with which to cleanse my wounds.

We hurried on for another 30 minutes to find a healer man who worked on broken bones. He patched my head with an herb and medicinal poultice and told my mother, "If this boy should by chance live to be ten years old, he is going to be blind or deaf because too many things literally came out of his head." In a few weeks I was healed and started getting my strength back. Despite that big gash in my head, the Lord healed me, though I still have some scars. I was expected to die, or be deaf and blind. Instead, at ten years old, I received a spiritual resurrection in my life. Besides, I never experienced any sight or hearing problems. The Lord made me completely whole from all infant injuries.

We grew up in rural mountains and not the city, so we were limited. I was better at volleyball than at soccer. My brothers and I planted gardens with corn, beans, and sweet potatoes among their produce.

I KNEW HOW TO GO WITHOUT

Growing up in Haiti with its daily hard scrabble realities was a good experience for it helped me to appreciate my current blessings. I don't hate nor am I in any way bitter about my humble beginnings for I was raised with a heart that God gave me. While I enjoy the good life, like 24 hour a day electricity, in the United States; I know how to make do with a little and do without a lot.

EARLY RESPECT FOR THE SUPERNATURAL

I respect the supernatural because, from an early age, I have seen God's power manifested. One incident that I witnessed, when only eight years old, instilled in me an early found respect for the supernatural. It was a physically manifested conviction from God's Holy Spirit. It was a time of revival and outpouring of God's Spirit at church. People were prophesying and speaking in tongues; messages and healings coming upon congregants gathering from all around the area for nonstop prayer. People were allowed just a few hours to go home and take care of necessary chores before being required to return to the ongoing service.

The men on one side and the ladies on the other side of the church were laying down, eyes closed, praying. The Holy Spirit was moving powerfully and so Dad got up and went to the men, some of whom were living in unmarried sin, although no one was aware of this. One of these out of wedlock couples were attending the meeting. He laid his hand upon the head of the man and it got stuck as if glued or cemented to it. He started walking toward the door and every move or bend he made; the man, like a bonded Siamese twin, would follow along. The door supernaturally opened before him and he dropped the man outside. Returning, he went to the woman of the sinful couple and put his hand on her head and she stuck too. He dropped the woman outside also and when she fell on the ground, she started screaming. Everyone shouted, "Look what is happening!" The couple confessed their sin and called their parents. Later they decided not to live in sin and got married. From that time, I had a great amount of respect for the supernatural power of God.

A SECRET REVEALED

Another time, when I was a child, all the grownups were away and only we children were at home. I took some bread to eat but didn't want anyone to know that I did. My parents came home about 11 o'clock and got up at two in the morning to sing and worship in tongues; a sweet melody unto the Lord. I heard my father say, "Don't blame that which is missing on others, Joel, Joel, Joel . . ." In other words, the Holy Spirit told them about my taking the bread. I was very chastened and frightened; knowing that God knew about my little bread napping and had revealed it to my Dad.

When I grew up, God wanted me to know that He is real and that I must trust Him and respect Him. I have seen many other miracles and greatly believe in the supernatural for it is real.

DEAD MAN RAISED TO LIFE

I remember another miracle which God performed through my Dad. As Dad was passing the home of a man who had just died, he saw the people mourning and crying. The Lord spoke to his heart to enter the house. In Haiti, when someone dies, especially in the mountains, all the rooms in the deceased persons home are emptied except for where the corpse lies in repose. Before they dressed and put him in the coffin to be taken to the cemetery my dad entered and asked permission to pray for the dead man. He prayed and then the Spirit told Dad to lay down on the corpse. Obedient to the Holy Spirit, he did just as instructed and blew into the dead man's nose and the deceased came back to life. This brought so much joy and a great example of God's power to this area that most of the people in that village gave their lives to the Lord. Since that miracle, Voodoo is minimal in that area because its inhabitants know the power of God.

CHAPTER 3

GROWING UP IN THE PROPHECY
God Would Do A Great Thing In Me

RECEIVING ETERNAL LIFE

When I was 10 years old a missionary came to my Dad's church and showed a T.L. Osborn miracle film called "Black Gold," filmed in Africa, where the Lord was healing thousands. Osborn was preaching to multitudes of Africans who were getting saved. All of a sudden, I heard myself praying, "Lord, I give my life to You! I like what this man is doing. I want to do this too when I grow up. I give my life to You. I want to ask You to forgive me of all my sins. I ask You to give me Your life and I will serve You all of my life!" My shirt was getting wet from crying. That very day I gave my life to the Lord and felt a change and a great joy. I know that at the very moment I gave my heart to the Lord my spirit was resurrected.

As a young, rambunctious boy, I used to fight a lot with other children. I would tease them and then tussle with them. I was a mean boy, even though I loved the Lord. As we were growing up my dad would teach us scriptures every day and we had to memorize them. We thought he was trying to kill us with scriptures but his diligent efforts to raise us up in God's word really helped us to this day.

PRAYER AND FASTING BROUGHT MIRACLES

In 1955, when I was 7 years old, the Holy Spirit came down in a mighty way and many extraordinary things began happening. I was just a little boy but I remember what it was like to receive permission to run home and do whatever chores needed to be done and then come back to church. The meeting was a permanent all day service.

People gathered together from all over to be healed; many had their teeth renewed. Lots of serious diseases were eliminated. The houses on our church grounds became spiritual healing clinics. People would arrive and stay for many days until they were healed. I saw lots and lots of miracles.

We fasted, drinking only water, three days every month from Thursday through Saturday to cleanse and prepare ourselves for communion service. People would come and just lie down, pray, read the Bible, prophesy and seek God's face and His wisdom. We had all night prayer meetings and worshipped in different places. It was a good time of revival.

PRAYER AND FASTING

We fasted, drinking only water, three days every month from Thursday through Saturday to cleanse and prepare ourselves for communion service. People would come, lie down, pray, read the Bible, prophesy, seek God's face and His wisdom. We conducted all night prayer meetings and worshipped in different places. It was a good time of revival.

In 1955 the Holy Spirit manifested in a mighty way and many extraordinary things began happening. I was just a little boy but I remember what it was like to receive permission to run home and do whatever chores needed to be done and then come back to church. The meeting was a permanent all day service. Lots of serious diseases were eliminated. I saw numerous miracles.

I START TO PREACH

When I was 12, I started preaching to, praying for and teaching my classmates at school. The scriptures really helped me to get started for it was good that I knew what to say. I used to get children from other schools to come to our Christian school to debate and compare what we and they knew. When it was my turn to speak, I always had plenty of scriptures and words to tell children about how Jesus said, "Let the children come to me" and then blessed them. There was a lot of applause for me because of the scriptures that I knew. It was a blessing to know the scriptures. We always helped our Dad do his work; breaking stones or building something. He had three big works to do; reading the Bible, teaching the Bible to us and preaching the Gospel to others. When at home, we were always learning how to do something productive with our hands, as well reading the Bible and witnessing God's word.

I was saved at the age of 12, the Lord filled me with the Holy Spirit and I started preaching in my Dad's church. When I was 13, there was need for a pastor in a small church at Marre Joffre. Every Sunday, my dad sent me to preach there and to pray for the people. I didn't know what was going on but just prayed and saw adults kneeling down and giving their hearts to the Lord. People were healed, demons cast out and many miracles happened in that church. The church flourished because there was a special anointing on the ministry which everyone was experiencing.

Henceforth, from the age of 13, I continued preaching. I was also responsible for a school at Marre-Rouge that was three hours away from our house. I had to walk there every morning and evening; three hours one way and three hours return.

I was a teacher and principal at that school despite being very young but I was respectful of the children and their parents. For about four years my life was spent doing that but as I was making my long perambulatory commutes, I was always joyful and thanking God for giving me the ability to do it.

After my time at Marre-Rouge I was engaged to teach at Oriani School which was a six-hour walk away and would do so back home every weekend. Some of the places where I had to go were very mountainous but I joyfully prevailed with God's help. Many of the children whom I taught in these outlying schools are still serving God. I was teaching and serving the Lord with what I knew, even though I was barely into high school myself, it helped that I was privileged to know how to read and write.

Upon completion of my call to teach I joined my Dad on his mission trips. Sometimes it would take us two days on foot and on horseback to travel from one place to another.

I also started preaching, teaching and praying for people in my Dad's church in Savane-Zombie, now called Canaan. There was a lot of applause for me because of the scriptures that I knew. It was a blessing to know the scriptures.

I once met a lady who knew me when I was a child and told me about the first sermon I ever preached in the church. It was on Matthew 11:28, "Jesus said to have the people who are tired and heavy laden, to come to him."

But my first preaching to the children in the school was Mark 10:13, "Suffer the little children to come unto me . . ."

God's Word has been important to me throughout my entire life.

1 Corinthians 15:58 says, "Therefore, my beloved brethren, be ye steadfast, un-moveable, always abounding in the work of the Lord, for as much as ye know that your labour is not in vain in the Lord."

THE BIBLE, OUR INHERITANCE

The time came for me to decide what I was to do with my life. I was now 18 years old. My dad told me that the only gift he wanted to give me was a Bible: "This Bible will take you places that you never dreamed you could go. It will put you in a position which you never dreamed you would be in. This is the inheritance that I can give you."

When it was time for my brother and me to make a decision, my Dad called us and said, "I have a plan for both of you. I want you to go into full-time ministry." To which my brother answered, "Well, we will come back and give you an answer."

So my brother and I went off to ponder on and discuss what Dad had suggested; "How in the world can we enter into full time ministry? What support will that give us? What can a Bible do for us?" we asked ourselves.

We went back to my father and told him, "We want to learn a trade or something so we are able to have a family and support a wife and children. We didn't want to be itinerant preachers like him roaming the mountain villages living hand to mouth, day by day. We wanted to have our own cars and homes."

Young Joel with Dad, Bishop Rameau D. Jeune

JONAH

Embracing my future life based on the bible did not excite me. How would I ever have a home, a car, a wife and all the blessings, in life that a person, who is not poor has?

Consequently, at the age of 16 I decided to run away; fleeing to a better life! Like Jonah in the bible I tried to run from my father and from God; running off to the mountains. I walked three hours chasing after a better life in the Dominican Republic. Almost there just across the border in Haiti; I stayed with some people in a Safe House used by others like me seeking a more prosperous life in the Dominican Republic.

Though my father had many others to look after, children, church members and more; he had a stirring deep inside, something was missing, something was not right; where was Joel? The promised son, the one raised from the dead to serve God; who would one day be a mighty man of God and help to deliver Haiti; Joel the one so musically talented, was missing.

Even though I would stay overnight with other friends or relatives from time to time, my father sensed, something was not right with Joel and he was determined to find me.

Oh no, I could hear his voice and footsteps, I tried to hide under the mattress I was sleeping on. How did he find my Safe house? Who told him I was there? The same Holy Spirit had revealed where I was to him and I couldn't hide. Only one night away from my dream of a new life away from the bible, poverty and church but I could not escape.

Bracing myself for the worst licking of my life, I was surprised that my dad met me with kindness and understanding instead. He actually understood and God changed my heart to serve him fully and find the prosperity and freedom I sought through His bible.

BIBLE SCHOOL DECISION

My father had told me, "God wants me to give you a Bible, the Bible; that's what your call is. That is your profession!" How could I make a living with that alone? Dad had taught me about faith and how God could use me in ministry and still take care of me; how He could impart His power unto me.

I prayed about it and finally agreed to accept the Bible as my inheritance. I was afraid to disobey my dad, so I told him, "Okay, I will go to Bible school." When I got there, I was the youngest among the students who teased me, chanting, "This Bible School is for children now." But the Lord helped me and I acclimated to life with the other students. I was assigned along with other students to mow the grass during the first semester.

I prayed to God, "Lord, I want you to teach me English and how to drive. In six months I want skills to translate and interpret, for the missionaries." Late at night, I began studying and the Lord taught me the English language. When I began conversing with the missionaries in English, they replied with surprise saying, "When and how did you learn English, Joel?" I told them that the Lord had helped me and so they changed my assignment to translating text and course books, from English to French.

I translated I Corinthians, II Corinthians, I and II Thessalonians, etc., and other books which were used in the Bible School curriculum. Once again the Lord heard my prayer and came through for me.

Called to Preach

LEARNING TO DRIVE

Learning to drive was another and very amusing miracle for me since I lived in the mountains. There were no bicycles in the hills, so like others, to these regions born, I had no experience with them. I only knew how to ride a horse, donkey or mule but it was my heart's desire to learn how to drive when I saw the big trucks passing by down the mountain toward the city.

I was about 16 years old when the idea of driving struck me. I shared my food with the operator of a big government dump truck working on the mountain. These were the only vehicles up there. I traded him my food for letting me learn how to turn the steering wheel. Some of my friends made fun of me, saying I was a servant to the driver. In turning that wheel for him I knew I was learning something.

Because of that experience the missionaries; at the seminary I was attending in Port au Prince, graciously allowed me to use the mission's car to practice driving. I learned to drive quickly because I already knew how to manipulate the wheels of the car; all I had to learn was how to operate the clutch and gears so in six months I received my driver's license and began to drive.

My family members were somewhat shocked but realized that from that humble and somewhat derided beginning in the dump truck I had progressed to be one of the few licensed drivers in our area. Once more God had opened opportunities for me to help achieve my goal. I am so thankful to the Lord.

STUDYING MUSIC

I also learned how to play piano and accordion and was talented in classical music. I learned how to read and write music and develop songs. While attending seminary I helped preach, lead worship and go on visitations to people in need.

God was teaching us pastoral skills there in Bible school. We were sent out to conduct Summer Vacation Bible School for children. We went out evangelizing, two by two, into many towns, villages and cities throughout Haiti. Because of those evangelism experiences, I know almost all of Haiti. The Bible school was a real blessing for me.

NO SHOES TO WEAR

I had many trials, often having nothing. I remember one time when the soles of my shoes were so worn out that my feet were touching the ground. Another time, Pastor Don Allen, the school director, asked me to go with him to a church in Belladere, a village in the mountains. The outreach would last all weekend.

I told him, "I have no decent shoes; the soles on my one pair are worn out. I can't go like this on the mission." He answered, "You can go! We will make sure that you do." The way he said it, I thought he was going to give me a new pair of shoes but he didn't and when everybody was ready, he told me, "Let's go!" I had no choice, so I just jumped into the old four wheel drive Land Cruiser Jeep with my clothes, my Holy Bible and my holy shoes and away we went. I prayed, "Lord, I want You to make a miracle for me, because I need some shoes."

Upon returning, on Monday morning, I was pleasantly surprised that one of my brothers, who was in Nassau, Bahamas, had sent me $15. At that time $15 was, to me, like $1,500 dollars. I used the unexpected gift to buy the nicest shoes that I had ever owned. I thank God that He willed me to go on that mission with my worn out shoes.

The Lord helped me out in many such ways until I graduated with honors as Valedictorian of my class. I didn't know what to do next, so I continued to reside at the school and prayed, "Lord, shall I go back to the mountains and work with my dad, or do you have something else for me?"

HARD TIMES AT BIBLE SCHOOL

In order to support myself at the school and help my mother, I had to go out every Saturday to find work. I learned how to mix cement, carry blocs and other skills and was paid $1.00 each day. I would buy emptied cement bags and fabricate grocery bags out of them to sell.

I was tempted many times to leave the Bible School. I went to factories and elsewhere but the doors for employment never opened for me.

MORE CHALLENGES AFTER GRADUATING FROM THE THEOLOGICAL SEMINARY

In 1970, after my graduation, the Seminary being on vacation break, there was no food available for me. I went to see one of my older brothers who owned a big house with a couple of vacant rooms and asked his wife if I could stay in their home for a short time. She hospitably offered me a room. My brother was away preaching for the weekend and returned in the middle of the night, his wife cheerfully announced that she had given me a room to stay in until the Lord would lead me in a new direction.

From my room I overheard my brother say, "No, he cannot stay in my house. I will not spend my money to feed him." His wife replied, "That's not a problem, he can do little jobs around here to provide for his food." My brother angrily replied, "No! He has to leave my house tonight!" His wife persisted, "All right, let's tell him to leave tomorrow morning, it's already midnight now." "No! Tonight," he insisted. I didn't wait to be told to leave but got up, folded my bed, took my belongings and walked out. I went back to the Seminary where I spent the rest of the night on the porch because everything was closed. I didn't get angry at my brother because I knew that the Lord was allowing me to be tested thus adding to my personal testimony.

Now I was back at the school having no money or job. Every day I prayed and asked God what to do? Mr. Lahens, one of the caretakers told me, "Joel, you are really going to know what hardship, misery and hunger are all about in the big city of Port-au-Prince. By faith, I answered, "In eight days God is going to do a miracle for me. God will give me a place to live, food to eat and a family to help me out."

Seven days after I spoke those hopeful words, while sitting on the dormitory porch steps, I observed a white Opel automobile arrive at the school. An American missionary was driving and stopped where I was sitting. He exited the car, walked up to me and asked, "Do you know a young man named Joel Jeune?" I replied, "Yes, I know him well, do you have a message for him?"

He answered, "I need to talk to him. Please call him for me, if he is available." I replied. "I am Joel Jeune and I am available." His next words were the answer to my prayers, "Can you come and live with my family? We will feed you, give you a home to live in; you will be my interpreter and Creole teacher to my family." I didn't hesitate, "Give me five minutes to gather up my stuff!"

His name was Pastor Morris Wilson from Topeka, Kansas. I became part of his family. I improved my English, became a teacher of four classes at their Bible School in Laboule and was their language interpreter.

This was the door God opened for me as I began my life journey. I was cared for very well working for and living with the Wilsons until they left Haiti.

NEW CHALLENGES AFTER THE WILSON'S LEFT HAITI

Quite suddenly, the Wilsons left Haiti and I was left homeless. My mother and sister had moved to Port-au-Prince and I was left to support them. With the little money my friends, the Wilsons left me, I rented a small 2 room house at Cité-Bau, on Delmas 6, Port-au-Prince and moved in with my mother and sister.

I continued to teach at the Bible School in Laboule which was managed now by two other missionaries, Mary and Hazel Shepherd from Oklahoma. My salary was $15 per month for teaching English and music classes. I was also their interpreter for 4 classes daily each week. I was responsible for paying my own transportation, which cost $8 per month and I was left with only $7 to take care of my family and other personal expenses.

I do not know how I paid the rent and made it every month but I know God miraculously provided for our needs.

BELIEVING GOD FOR EVERYTHING

I started believing God for everything that I needed. Even when I was going to get married, I had to believe God for my provision. I've seen many of His teachings on faith come alive in my life. I've observed many great happenings, because He told me, "By accepting Me (Jesus), trusting Me, believing Me and remaining faithful to My purpose for your life; you will be surprised what I, the Lord, can do for you." I continue to witness these things happening!

AMERICA: THE DREAM LAND

One more thought I remember often repeated was to come to the United States. I said, "Lord, I will come back to Haiti." But in my mind I realized that if I went to the United States, I would never want to go back to Haiti. I tried seven times but each time I was denied a visa at the US Embassy. I remember, very clearly, the last time I was denied.

Before I went to the embassy, I implored my mother, "Please fast for me. Don't eat or drink or do anything. Just stay and pray until I return with the visa." I went to the embassy confident that I would get a visa but when I got there, they told me, "No sir, you are too young; without a wife, house or anything established to bring you back to the country." I assured them, "I will come back." Their answer was still, "No!" I returned, disappointedly, to my mother's home. When I got there, I found my mother was not praying. She had already finished the fast because she thought that by 12 o'clock I would have received my visa. I asked her, "Mom, why are you not praying? I asked you to pray until I got back!" She replied, "I thought you already got it."

No, I did not get it and I was going to kill myself; so I just took off. I didn't know where I was going but on my way, I encountered a small church, alongside the road, with no walls, just a little roof made of tree leaves. I went inside of it out of the heat of the day. I told myself, "Before I die, let me have a few minutes to rest here." So I laid down on the ground and put my feet up on a bench and fell asleep.

I had a wonderful dream of what God had in store for me; I saw a big crowd of people and lots of leaders. I saw myself going places. The Lord confronted me and all of this was happening in Haiti. I realized that the Lord had something special for me in Haiti and this changed my desire to live in the United States. I was willing to remain in Haiti, no matter what might happen there.

The revelation that God gave me was to remain in Haiti; get busy with God's work and watch him bless me.

I felt a call to preach. God called me for Haiti and removed my desire to go live in the United States. I know there have been prophecies on my life, before I was a pastor. The prophecies were saying that I would be a Bishop over many churches. I didn't want to hear them.

CHAPTER 4

God's Helpmate

"BUT I'M JUST A CHILD!"

I first noticed girls when I was about 15 years old while I was already in the ministry. After graduating from Bible school which closed for vacation break I had to make a decision to go back to my mountain village or stay in town. I felt that God had something new in store for me.

Brother Morris Wilson, had a nice place arranged for me and invited me to stay there. The food and lodgings were good and everything was taken care of. I began praising God and teaching him and his children Creole and interpreting in the Bible School that he was associated with. I taught four classes at the school. We became very good friends and worked well together. He loved me very much.

While staying at the Bible school and teaching, it became necessary for me to get married. Being a young eligible man, the girls were "looking" at me. Nearly a dozen of them approached me and said they had dreamed about my becoming their husband.

So I asked the Lord for a wife and prayed seriously about that. God showed me Doris (nicknamed "Guerly") in a dream. I had never met her but saw her face and heard the way she talked in that dream. I shared this with Brother Wilson and he said, "Okay, I will pray with you."

Prior to my dream I approached him and said, "Brother Wilson, how would you feel if you were a young man like me: a man without a home, a wife, a family or a job; with nothing to live for. Wouldn't you feel like killing yourself?"

He answered my sorrow, "How were you last year? Were you better or worse?" I replied, "I believe I have more now than last year." He continued, "Why don't you believe God that next year and the future will be better? I will believe with you, that God will remove this depression from your mind."

He knew some of the girls in Bible school who were looking at me. That was not my desire. Three months later, he came and told me, "The person whom you described in your dream, I think I have met her." I said, "Yeah, really!" I was excited to see whom he had found.

He took me to the Gospel Crusade orphanage at Delmar 75. The lady that was overseeing it was Helen Nichols from Connecticut; who later became Helen Valme and now lives in San Antonio, Texas. She was a friend of Brother Wilson and had invited him and some missionaries to the girls' home where he met Doris L. Burke.

Later he took me too meet her. She was only 16 and seeing her I said, "Lord, this is not her. This girl is too small." However, before I left, I saw her talking to another girl and heard her voice. I said, "That's her!" Her voice convinced me that she was the one whom I had seen in my dream.

To meet with her was very difficult. I went to Helen and told her what the Lord showed me. To meet with Sister Helen was not easy, either. Being the Administrator and housemother for more than 70 children kept her very busy. I came to the orphanage more than seven times trying to meet with her, to no avail. Telephones were not yet available in the country; so I couldn't call her. Sometimes I would wait in the church yard for more than five hours. Many of the children would come out and ask me, "What do you want Mom Helen to do for you? We have seen you here all the time waiting for her." Finally, after waiting more than three hours one day, I met with Mom Helen and Doris as they returned to the orphanage after shopping for their house.

I was confident that she was the girl but was told, "She is only 16 and is not interested now." "That's impossible," I said, "okay, I will let the Lord talk to you about that."

Three months later, Mom Helen sent word to tell me that the Lord let her know that this indeed is what He wanted for Guerly, who knew nothing about this revelation. When told about this she got angry, "No, I am not interested, I am a child!, said Guerly.

Finally, I went to their church, located next to the children's home, and asked the piano player to teach me how to play so I could have another reason to return. I frequented the church twice a week; hoping to see and talk to her myself but that never happened. Guerly refused to talk with me; so, one day, Sister Helen got her and said, "Let's go talk to him." Guerly declined this request but Mom Helen insisted until she obeyed and went along with her. I saw them coming, so I just pretended to be playing the piano.

The first thing I said to her was, "Are you afraid of me?" Upon hearing this she loudly replied: I am not afraid of you, but I don't know who you are and I am not interested in knowing who you are.

It took about six months for her to talk and pray with me; after which she told me that God had His hand on our situation.

Doris (Guerly) and Joel when they first met

Two years later, while we were planning on getting married, Brother Wilson and his family departed Haiti. Mary and Hazel Shepperd were the new missionaries who replaced the Wilsons and now I was working with them. They were very unhappy about me getting married; telling me I was not financially ready to do it, knowing that my only income was $15 dollars a month.

BELIEVING GOD FOR EVERYTHING

I started believing God for everything that I needed for the wedding. I bought some used furniture from my older brother Leonard. Pastor Dan and his wife Donna Deaton had given us a house to stay in and pastor a church in Vigner Arcahaie. They also gave us their used motorcycle and an old car.

Even the very day, at the age of 24, when I was going to get married, I had to believe God for my financial provision. I spent the whole day trying to find $15 to go pick up my wedding suit from the tailor. The wedding was scheduled for 6 pm and it was a little before 5pm when I finally got a $20 gift from my friend Pastor Constant Pierre, an Assembly of God pastor. I ran to pick up my suit but was one hour late for my own wedding but well dressed and God blessed.

Guerly had been patiently waiting at the church for more than an hour when I arrived but the pastor who was solicited to perform the wedding became impatient and left. Another Pastor stepped in and performed the ceremony.

Doris L. Burke ("Guerly") and I were married and God opened a new life for both of us. Our God is so faithful! He is our Jehovah Jireh! I got married because that is what God wanted me to do and I thank God for my family, all of whom are serving the Lord. I thank God for my wife Doris who is beside me all the time. She is always doing something and is a blessing to the ministry and to Haiti. Doris Jeune exceeds the Proverbs 31 requirements of a good woman.

We were not able to go away for a honeymoon, so we moved to the church in Vigner the same night of the wedding. We have been living a honeymoon since that day, more than 40 years ago.

God is so good! We've seen many of His teachings on faith come alive in our lives. I've observed many great happenings, because He told me, "By accepting Me (Jesus), trusting Me, believing Me and remaining faithful to My purpose for your life; you will be surprised what I, the Lord, can do for you." I continue to witness these wonders happening!

It took many years for us to understand why the Lord let me go through so much and be late for my own wedding. All things work for good to them who love God, and being called according His purpose.

Married at 24 and 18 years old

In spite of my work schedule, I do my best to keep the spark of romance alive. It helps that we are always traveling together; doing the television programs and making decisions together. Doris oversees the orphanage and the school; I oversee the spiritual ministry. We communicate regularly; deciding together on what needs to be done. God has blessed us with unity. Traveling together helps us to stay in marital, romantic and unbreakable relationship.

I have to believe God will lead me in every step I must take. We set our priorities according to our needs and the Lord's directions. We pray that God will stop us from doing anything He does not want us to do or that might be destructive to ourselves or the ministry. God continues to do that for us.

Bishop Rameau, Doris and Joel

Dad was always there for us, to help in every difficult moment of our marriage, but I had to believe God to lead me in every next step I must take. We set our priorities according to our needs and the Lord's directions.

We pray that God will stop us from doing anything He does not want us to do or that might be destructive to ourselves or the ministry. God continues to do that for us.

CHAPTER 5

Early Days

BUILDING GOD'S KINGDOM

The first few years of marriage were a little difficult. When we first married, we went to a church out of town, called Vigner Arcahaie. I first went to Vigner to interpret for Pastor Dan Deaton from Ohio. He and his wife pastored that church. I would travel from Port-au-Prince twice a week to interpret. When they were ready to leave Haiti, they asked me to pastor the church. The same night my wife and I got married, we moved to Vigner. Thank God for the Deaton family who gave us our very first motorcycle and a small car.

We only spent three months there. The water, a creek flowing beside the road was badly polluted. Two miles upstream people were bathing, washing clothes; cows and donkeys were drinking and more so we had to boil the water to try to purify it. We did not have the money to buy safe, purified water to drink. After three months, my wife got so sick we thought she was going to die. She could not take it there so we moved back to Carrefour, where I began pastoring a small church. We lived on one side while the church was on the other end of a house rented by a group called World Ministry Outreach. We pastored there for a year and a half. We also started "Faith Bible School" training leaders for the Kingdom. I was the only teacher since I had no financial means to hire other teachers. With God's miraculous provision we were able to feed bread and juice to the students every day.

COMING TO THE UNITED STATES THE VISA MIRACLE

The way God opened the door for us for travel to the United States is amazing. Before I got married, I was turned down 7 times with a red mark indicating that I would never be granted a visa to visit the United States. God always makes a way where there is none.

While pastoring the church in Arcachon, somebody came and asked us if we would like to volunteer as interpreters on a U.S Army Hospital Ship coming to Port-au-prince, to give medical assistance to the Haitian people. Our quick answer was yes. My wife and I donated 2 weeks of our time and services interpreting for the doctors and patients. With God's help we accomplished such a good job that we were highly favored over all other interpreters on the Ship and became the Captain's personal interpreters. In order to show his great appreciation to us the Captain asked us if there was anything we would like him to help us with? My heart jumped inside of me: "We are so glad that you asked". "We would like you to help us get a visa to travel to the United States for 2 months", we answered. "Do both of you already have a passport"? He asked. "Yes sir, we do". "Bring your passport tomorrow morning; I'll take you to the Embassy to get your visa." "Yes Sir, thank you very much" we replied. That night, we could hardly sleep.

We arrived at the ship very early in the morning. The Captain took us to the Embassy in his official VIP limousine, with no appointment, in less than 15 minutes we had the visa in our passports along with an apology from the Consulate General. Thank God! The closed door had been opened.

There were a few more challenges such as money for the plane tickets and my wife's 8 month pregnant condition. Women at this advanced stage of pregnancy are not ordinarily allowed to travel on commercial airplanes. Our God of miracles provided the travel money through Pastor Gerald Derstine and Leslie and Fern Helman. The day of departure my wife and I prayed, checked in at the airport counter, walked through the passenger line and boarded the Pan American airplane and nobody objected.

The Lord had opened the door to visit the United States. So we flew to Miami, our first time in an airplane; a dream come true. Who said you will never be blessed, delivered, healed, prosperous, married and have children? Which report are you going to believe?

His word says: "I will bless thee and make thy name great; and thou shalt be a blessing." Gen.12:2. "I will make my covenant between me and thee, and will multiply thee exceedingly. Gen. 17:2. "Behold, I have set before thee an open door, and no man can shut it." Rev.3:8. When men say it's over for you, God says it's new beginning for you.

CULTURE SHOCK IN THE UNITED STATES

Our first time in an airplane was a shock, but the greatest surprises were the electronic doors and escalators at the Miami airport. I thought these stairs were moving by magic because nobody ever told me about all these electronic wonders. The overpasses, bridges and highways were great shocks to both of us. It took us a couple of weeks to realize we were not in a dream.

However, after a month in the United States we wanted to return home because the desire of our hearts was for Haiti.

Doris was now 9 months pregnant, our first child was due and we wanted him to be born in America.

While we agonized over staying or leaving, my assistant pastor back home wrote us that somebody had purchased the church and house property, in Haiti, where we lived and ministered. We had no physical space to go back to. Despite this difficult reality we wanted to go home to Haiti.

A MIRACLE IN BRADENTON, FLORIDA

Our next miracle happened in Bradenton, Florida on 17th Avenue. We were staying at Leslie and Fern Helman's house located on 21st Avenue in Bradenton. Every day I took my wife for a walk and encouraged her to jump a few times to stimulate the baby to be birthed sooner as we had such a burning desire to go back to Haiti.

We heard about a tent revival service and on our daily walk, we went, out of curiosity, to see what was going on. The tent was the largest we had ever seen as was the crowd inside it. The service was presided over by an evangelist from Maryland named W. DeLate.

We needed prayer for our homeless in Haiti challenge and Brother Delate prayed for all who expressed needs to be met. We joined the prayer line.

He asked us what our need was. I told him "We are from Haiti, are expecting a baby and we have lost our home and church location as the property was sold." "What part of Haiti are you from?" he asked us. I said, "Port-au-Prince." "What part of Port-au-Prince?" he asked. I said, "Carrefour." "What street in Carrefour?" By that time, we thought this man was asking too many questions. We said, "Arcachon 32." He asked, "What house?" We told him what house.

It was now his house for he had just bought it. He told us we could live in the house until we found something else. This was such a great, supernatural miracle for us. God led us directly to him. Praise God we didn't have to worry about a place to live. We returned to Haiti to our church and home with our new born son Jonny, who was then 10 days old and stayed in that house until the purchase of the new property at Waney 93, Carrefour, with the help of Gospel Crusade and Papa Abe Hostetler of Plain City, Ohio, Pastor Richard Brown and the late Henry Brunk. We are thankful for their great contribution towards the purchase of this property.

OUR FAMILY AND CHURCH BEGIN

The Lord blessed me with my wonderful wife Doris, who is a wonderful helpmate, hard worker, faithful friend and dedicated minister of the Gospel.

Joel and Doris Jeune

Behind Joel Jeune and the Holy Spirit there is a powerful Doris Burke Jeune that's instrumental in the success of all the ministry God has given us to do.

After two years of marriage we were blessed with Jonny, our first child, born in Bradenton.

OUR FOUR SONS AND ONE DAUGHTER

God blessed us with four wonderful, healthy and happy sons and led my wife and myself to adopt a very special daughter.

(From back to front) Joel, Doris, Joel-Helman, Jonny, Danny, Michael,

Joanne age 5

Joanne at 16 years old

Jonny J., Joel Helman, Danny J., and Michael Rameau Jeune.

Jonny, Michael and Danny were all born in Manatee Memorial Hospital, Bradenton, Florida. Joel was born in Harrisburg, Pennsylvania. Joanne our daughter was born and adopted in Haiti.

When our children were young, it was hard on them because we were gone so often. At vacation time we would travel with the boys, talking with them that they might understand the importance of our traveling for the survival of the ministry. One cannot isolate oneself, in Haiti, if all the needs for the ministry work are to be met.

My times with our four boys are filled with many memorable and cherished moments. I remember when my first son, Jonny, was sitting on a chair beside the pulpit looking up and listening to me preach.

We thank the good Lord for our sons and daughter and all the people who support us financially, help us physically and advice us wisely. All the GLORY be to GOD.

Now that our sons are all grown up, they have been making the burden much lighter for us by giving much of their time, knowledge, skill and talents in the building of God's kingdom in Haiti.

The oldest is Jonny J. Jeune, born in 1974. He lives in Miami with his wife Daphney Civil Jeune and their sons Jonathan and Joshua. He is a civil engineer; involved in all manner of building projects. Jonny loves God very much and serves Him in all he does. Making frequent trips to Haiti and is responsible for Grace's empowerment program; the sustainable community project and housing construction to restore the lives of the thousands of earthquake victims.

Joel Helman Jeune is our second son. He is a graduate of Oral Roberts University with a degree in business administration and is very active in the church. We thank God for him. He has taught at the high school level.

Danny J. Jeune studied law and criminal justice in college graduating from Harding University in Arkansas. He wanted to be a professional basketball player and spent four years playing basketball in France. He and his wife Stephanie moved from Colorado to Miami, Fla. for a time. They are both involved in education and lead the International Club of Friendships (ICOF), caring for children and needy people in Haiti, Africa and other countries around the world.

Michael Rameau Jeune, born in 1981, is our fourth son. He graduated from Southeastern University in Lakeland, Florida and received his Master's Degree in music, majoring in opera, at the University of Georgia. He sings, is very musically talented and has a vocal ensemble. He was a semi-finalist on the "American Idol" television program. He also took classes at Harvard University. He is now happily married to his childhood sweetheart Luce Andral and together, living in Haiti, they are continuing full time the work at Grace Village.

(Back row)Danny, Stephanie, Michael, Joel-Helman, Daphney, Jonny Jeune (Front) Doris & Joel Jeune

Joanne & Mommy Doris Jeune

Now grown up, Joanne J. Jeune is studying nursing in Haiti. We're looking forward to her loving help in our ministry to the people of Haiti.

Pastor Doris and I wish all of our sons and our daughter will be involved in the ministry of spreading the Gospel to others but I don't know yet who God will call. We hope all of our children will become full time ministers.

Proud Grand-Pa & Grand-ma Jeune

We are so proud of Naelle, Soley, Jonathan, Joshua our grandchildren.

The Lord put in my heart not to stay in the States, but to return to Haiti, take care of the ministry and build His Kingdom.

CHURCH GROWTH EXPERIENCE

We began our ministry at Waney, with open air meetings on our front porch. The space was too small so we broke down a wall in the servant's quarters, a small building behind our home, and began having church services there.

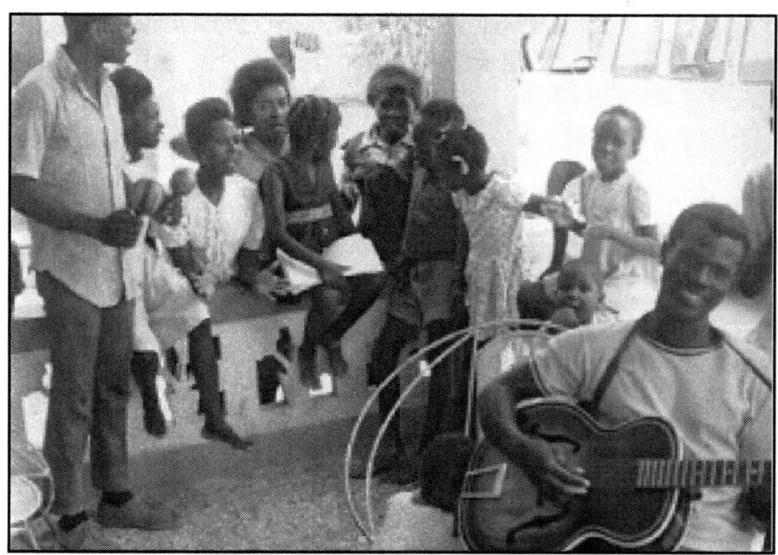

Our First Church Congregation under my Porch at Waney, Carrefour.

We started a school with 53 children, in that little 15 x 25 foot building. That first day, during devotions, 18 children gave their lives to Jesus. These children not only became the first members of the new church, they also brought their parents, brothers and sisters to get saved.

Our First School at Waney in 1975

The Lord blessed the school and in a short time it grew to many hundreds of students and great Christian teachers. Through the support of Grace Chapel and many others we built a very beautiful 2 story school building. All the glory be to God.

Waney School; Principal, Teachers and Student Body

The number of congregants rapidly increased beyond the capacity of our space. It became necessary to have a larger church building and we had no money to buy land or a building. So we decided to build our new church directly in front of our home. By faith we began digging for a foundation not knowing where money, for the construction materials, would come from. Dick and Joyce Helman, from Ohio, came to visit. Upon finding out that we had no materials to build with, they gave us money to buy the first load of sand and cement; what a real, genuine blessing!

We asked our church community to donate a cinder block or some other building material. I remember, in particular, Sister Faveur Yacinthe who brought us 12 cement blocks. With what had been donated we began building the foundation. Gospel Crusade Grace Chapel, Pastor Richard Brown of Tarpon Springs, Florida, Good News in Action of Dick and Joyce Helman and a couple of other churches helped us financially and we built the church. Praise God! In a few months, the church had its roof on and we commenced having services in a bigger church. All too soon, the new church building was full, to overflowing.

"Seek ye first the Kingdom of God, and His righteousness; and all these things shall be added unto you." Matt.6:33

I am a builder. My goal has always been: building God's Kingdom, not my own kingdom. I have never wanted to build a monument to myself. There is a constant need for expansion. Sometimes we don't finish (stucco and paint) a building. It is more important for us to meet the need for space, than to complete our structures smooth and beautiful. We hope to do so but it never happens because the need for more space is so great.

We extended the church twice. We divided it six times and we made seven other satellite churches emanating out of that original church. That was the beginning of 3 to 4 years of church construction.

With much prayer, teaching of the Word of God, evangelism, faith and God's miracles the church, at Waney, rapidly grew to many thousand members and now has more than to 4,000 regular members.

Our church grew to many thousands

Now, at the various locations, we are able to serve thousands of church members and people in the community.

Today we oversee and coordinate 270 churches and 70 schools. Many of these churches and schools are founded by Gospel Crusade of Haiti, some of them were planted by my father from Mission Eglise de Dieu Sainte Cité, and my wife and I have started some and others came to affiliate with our ministry. This is a network of churches. We thank the Lord for His strength and wisdom that He gave to us. Eventually with a lot of help from our friends we built a church on that foundation and called it Grace Tabernacle.

Our first church building at Waney in 1976.

BAD ECONOMIC SITUATIONS

Our main problem has been finances. The economy in Haiti was and is very bad. In the beginning we had very few contacts to get financial help. We were very small. Few believed in us or what was going to happen in our future. We were young, with very little experience. People, who might help, did not know if they could trust us. All we had was a vision and faith in God. We really needed to believe God and use everything we had to build our ministry until we started proving ourselves; then others would trust, assist, and help us more.

We broke that ground and started doing more for God until we attained our current status and respectability.

CHAPTER 6

Gods Army Of Love

Jesus came and spake unto them, saying: "All power is given to me in heaven and in earth. Go ye therefore, and teach all nations, baptizing them in the name of the Father, and the Son, and of the Holy Ghost: Teaching them to observe all things whatsoever I have commanded you: and lo, I am with you always, even unto the end of the world." Amen. Matt. 28:18-20

> **"When thou passest through the waters, I will be with thee; and through the rivers, they shall not overflow thee: when thou walkest through the fire, thou shalt not be burned; neither shall the flame kindle upon the." Isaiah 43:2**

When we started our ministry, all we had was God's promise. We had absolutely no promise of support from anybody else. However, it didn't take long before God start sending good people our way. Everything God allowed us to accomplish for Him is done only by miracles. Every great work we do for God always started with just our God given vision and our faith. By experience with God I can, very confidently and very proudly say: God never fails in His promises. He is faithful and able.

HELP FROM MANY CARING PEOPLE WHO BELIEVED IN US AND OUR VISION

One of our main problems has been finances. The economy in Haiti was and is very bad. In the beginning we had very few contacts to get financial help. Now we can confidently say that we have 'GOD'S ARMY OF LOVE' with us. We are so thankful for that.

We thank God for Gospel Crusade, Christian Retreat and Brother Gerald and Sister Beulah Derstine. While on a visit to Haiti they found my wife Doris (affectionately, in her childhood, called Guerly) in an orphanage, founded by Doris Burke, a Jamaican lady. Sister Burke took Guerly in when she was 5 days old and bestowed her own name on the little girl. Guerly's birth parents, desperately poor, like so many others in Haiti were unable to raise her and as others do, gave her up for adoption.

However the orphanage was so poor and so many of the children were dying that, through Gospel Crusade, Inc. the Derstines, Henry Brunk, Abe Hostetler, the Helmans and others; the Derstines provided care for and built a new home for the children. My future wife was their favorite sponsored child.

After we got married, they helped us get a home where we started our ministry. They also helped with purchasing a church and school. Gospel Crusade was the first one to join with us and our vision.

We came under the umbrella of Gospel Crusade. Pastor and Mrs. Gerald Derstine and Mr. and Mrs. Leslie Helman helped us to come to the United States.

At that time my wife was pregnant with our first son, Jonny Jeune; they helped us to have our baby at Bradenton, Florida.

Grace Chapel, with Pastor Luke Weaver Sr., helped us to purchase a piece of land across from our church making it possible to build a school and begin a feeding program supported to this day by Grace Chapel Church and Village Light House with Pastor Luke Jr. of Canada. This great work helped our church in Haiti. That is why we call our church Grace Tabernacle.

In our early days, Abe Hostetler greatly assisted us. We had Richard Brown who helped us in the construction of the school and first church. Our good friends Dick and Joyce Helman were always willing and able to aid us in our needs. We fondly remember Leslie and Fern Helman, their parents. Child Rescue services, an organization by Glen and Vanis Phillips blessed us abundantly. In addition some individual churches aided our efforts.

T.L. OSBORN PARTICIPATES

T. L. and Daisy Osborn received me at their office in Tulsa, Oklahoma when I first visited the United States in 1974. They had breakfast with me, gave me a tour at Oral Roberts University, bought nice shoes and a suit for me and dresses to send for my wife. They blessed me with a sound system, megaphones, soul wining books, miracle films, and a movie projector to bring back to Haiti and be used to get the fire of revival moving in my country.

T.L. Osborn with Joel R. Jeune in 1975.

LaDonna Osborn delivering a new suit and evangelism supplies to Joel Jeune to go reach Haiti for Jesus.

PASTOR BILLY JOE DAUGHERTY

Pastor Billy Joe Daugherty of Victory Christian Center, Tulsa, Oklahoma, came and helped us with big crusades. He was a great, ongoing supporter of our ministry in Haiti for many years, always faithful. He established and supported the Victory Bible Institute (VBI) on our Mission compound in Carrefour where hundreds of leaders have been trained, equipped and sent out to serve God.

R. W. SCHAMBACH

We honor R. W. Schambach, who held the first big crusade in the country of Haiti and fed thousands of our citizens.

World renowned Evangelist R.W. Schambach came to Haiti for a major crusade in 1983; of which I was the chairman. The Lord helped me to organize the largest crusade that Haiti has ever known. More than 100,000 people filled Sylvio Cator

Soccer Stadium in Port-au-Prince. We had to tell people via a radio broadcast that even standing room was dangerously overcrowded. It was amazing what God did during that crusade where many miracles took place.

R.W. Schambach, Haiti Crusade with Pastor Joel Jeune in 1983

Over 100 thousand in attendance nightly at the Soccer Stadium. Every day God bestowed many powerful miracles upon the people.

WE'RE GRATEFUL TO SO MANY

We are grateful to Pastor Henry Brunk and Pastor Gerald Derstine, Abe Hostetler, and Pastor Richard Brown all of whom supported us in various ways including the purchase of the Waney Church property. Pastor Phil and Sue Tasker, Dr. Ben and Ann Decker and Pastor James Fresh from St. Mark's Lutheran Church who brought Pastor Billy Joe Daugherty and Victory Christian Center all of whom led work teams to help us in the early years.

Wings of Victory International of St. Petersburg and Clearwater, Florida with George and Barbara Ragland have supported the children's feeding program for many years. They financially contributed and worked with us for more than four years on the Children's Hospital project at Carrefour, Haiti. We thank Trinity Broadcasting Network's countless television viewers who partnered with Paul and Jan Crouch to assist us with food and our Haitian television program for many years, until May of 2006. TBN's television audience assisted us through their generous financial donations, specifically earmarked (along with many other contributors from all across North America) toward the construction of "Grace Haiti Pediatric Hospital" at our Grace Village compound in Carrefour Haiti.

Kenneth Copeland, through Gil Tobias, his TV producer, contributed towards the purchase of land on which the girls' orphanage in Carrefour is built.

Haiti Love and Faith Ministries, based in Kansas, USA also played a major role in the support process for the girls' orphanage. They constructed the orphanage girls' residence and Lamentin school buildings. We thank Dr. Ted and Dorothy Grimes, as well as Haiti Faith and Love board members for their many years of outstanding leadership.

A committee in Pennsylvania operating under the covering of the Family Residential Services led by Bill and Carolyn Moore and Ken Snowden manages a sponsorship program for the boys' home. We are also thankful to Pastor Lee Miller and his church in Kokomo, Indiana; Clint and Leanne Miller, Dale and Vickie Halteman and other Board members for many years of excellent service and support. They bring a team into Haiti, twice a year to work at the Boy's Home and at Marlene Alix's orphanage in Jacmel.

We are also grateful to Helen Rogish, who helped our children for many years and took many medical teams into the mountains of Haiti.

We are thankful to Tom Connell, who introduced us to Christ Community Church in Camp Hill, Pennsylvania, under the leadership of Pastor Dave Hess, has been supporting us for many years.

Tom Connell also introduced me to Promise Keepers with whom,representing Haiti, I attended the One Million Man March on Washington.

'Christ for the Nations', many years ago, helped monetarily to build a church at Fond-Verrettes in the mountains, for our ministry.

Victory World Outreach of Norcross, Georgia helps monthly! Pastor Dennis Rouse held pastor's seminars for us.

Pastor Roy Allebach, Pennridge Tabernacle, Pennsylvania, has greatly contributed to purchasing the mission's property in Lamentin. They have also supported children in the school.

The Branch Fellowship in Pennsylvania with Pastor's Bob Kratz and Craig Bishop have also helped purchase the mission's property and encouraged mission teams to come and bless Haiti.

Gospel Crusade of Canada, with Pastor David Gingrich, always plays a great role in bringing teams from Canada to bless Haiti; to build and support many Haitian schools and has brought work teams which built the church at Bois-Caiman.

Rev. Luke Weaver, Jr. of Village Lighthouse Benton Pentecostal Church, in New Brunswick, Canada, has assisted in feeding our Haitian children in their school for many years. They bring work teams every year to build and equip churches and schools; also to work on the Grace Haiti Pediatric Hospital.

We're thankful for the Fellowship of Believers, in Sarasota, Florida, for many years of faithful support.

Thanks to Fish Creek Community Church in Wisconsin with Pastor Fred Miller which has been supporting our work in Haiti for many years. We are also thankful to Dr. Ben and Ann

Decker, as well as George and Annette Erickson for their long time friendship and support.

Thanks be to God for the Good News in Action Ministries with Joyce and John Snowden for many years of faithful support of the Haiti Children's Feeding Program, and for helping with the Ladies Seminars every year among their many other great efforts. Child Rescue Services from Sidney, Ohio have also supported us for many years.

Words of Life Church, under Pastor Stan Moore, in Miami, Florida, has helped to underwrite many of our annual children's Christmas parties, we could not do these parties without them!

We thank God for Marlon and Jerri Migala who, for many years, have been such a great blessing to the children of Haiti. Their Abba International Puppets Ministry, which for many years produced children's television programs for us and stages the "Story of Jesus Birth" as the centerpiece of our Annual Children's Christmas Party. Marlon and Jerri have rounded up and brought thousands of new toys to Haiti for many years, to give every boy and girl their own gift, during the Christmas Program. They bless many thousands of children in Haiti. Marlon, in his "Word-Smith" professional capacity, also co-wrote, edited and indexed this book. He continues to bless us as resident Word-Smith and Media Director as well as Public Relations Representative for Grace International working in our Miami Gardens offices. Sister Jerri manages our Miami Gardens office coordinating the various departments and being a prayer warrior always.

We acknowledge Vision Haiti with Pastor Gerald and Evangelist Paul Clerié for active participation in the Bois-Caiman spiritual warfare and their support of many school children in Bois-Caiman for many years.

Thanks also to Dr. Pat Bailey Jones Ministry for its outstanding contribution in helping to build the Elderly Widow's Home and for taking young men and women to train them in her school in the United States. We also thank Pastor Phil Derstine and the Christian Retreat Family Church for helping with the construction and support of the Widow's Home.

We thank God for great friends and supporters like: Pastor Bill Winston, Pastor Dave and Debbie White, Joe and Jane Ford,

Apostle Thelma Knowles and her great church called Lively Stones, Marvin and Kim Rindler, Meron Abraha, Warren and Suzanne Schreier, Jonny Jeune and for all our other friends, ministries and everyone else who supports the ministry in Haiti. We are grateful to all of them for their faithful sacrifice. We would not be able to accomplish God's work without their help and support.

ACCOMPLISHING FOR GOD

Praise God for His wisdom and His plan. He promised that through me, He would do a great work in Haiti, starting from nothing, to what God has done now. God is great and faithful. When we first started, I had only a vision and faith in God. We started with a small church, went on to a bigger one and the ministry continued growing.

CHALLENGES AND AMAZING MIRACLES

The Lord has helped me! Slowly, He started to bless the work. In the beginning there were no funds to build the church and school or pay the teachers but then the Lord showered us with abundant help to see us through the hardships and to accomplish his purpose for us.

I remember one of the miracles the Lord did for me. One time when I had my last provision, about fifty cents; somebody came to my house needing some food. We had no food left to offer, so I gave him that last 50 cents. I took my old, beat up motorcycle (I did not have a car then) for a drive and ran out of gas. By faith, I was trying to urge the motorcycle to start, bent over in prayer and when I lifted my head, I saw Rev. James Beatty from Cleveland, Ohio. He said, "What are you doing here?" I admitted, "Well, my motorcycle broke down. I am trying to make it go because I don't want to leave it on the street." He gave me some money and took me to buy some gas and to buy rice and beans for the children. So, when I seeded my 50 cents, God multiplied that blessing many times over for us. The miracle was that Brother Beatty was walking around looking for someone to help him find my house. He was about to give up when he discovered me with my out of gas motorcycle.

DEAD BABY RISES UP

God performs supernatural miracles so frequently in Haiti. We have witnessed more than we could possibly share in this book. One of the miracles that God did was in 1981, while I was preaching in my church. I saw that 6 or 7 people were entering church carrying a baby. They were crying and looked so depressed. Usually, I don't interrupt my message to pray for people but I did this time and took the girl in my arms to pray for her thinking she was just very sick I felt no life in her. When I prayed for her, she raised her head alive. I gave the child to her mother. Afterwards, I was told that she had been dead for four hours. An ambulance had been called to come and get her lifeless body. God, once again, performed a miracle. Her name is Mary Flore, she was raised in our home, became a bank teller in Carrefour and to this day she always testifies how she was dead and how God brought her back to life.

PREACHING MY CONSCIENCE

Once, as I was preaching, on the radio, against the mixture of Catholicism, Voodoo and witchcraft; I referred to Elijah and a fire that descended on his offering and the 400 Witch Doctors who were killed by Elijah. I said, "There is fire in touching God's people." Upon hearing this, the mayor of the city of Port-au-Prince, through his police chief, sent four men to come and get me. As soon as they got near my office, I was told by people who had witnessed seeing both front tires of their car spinning off the wheels to each side of the road and the Jeep dropping immobile on the road. The men just ran away leaving a letter ordering their, aborted, mission from the mayor. The next day I visited the chief. I heard how they were beating on people in some of the cells. Upon hearing of this, God gave me a boldness to take a stand and tell them how Voodoo is killing our country. Immediately the power of God came upon them and the men were convicted of their inhumanity.

The police chief told me I was free to leave. As I departed, being a young preacher, I prophesied like an Elijah "Because of all this torture that is going on here, the Lord is going to send fire upon this place." About one week later, the police had a problem with one part of the Haitian army who came to the jail house and shot it up; causing a fire to burn the building. The police to whom I had witnessed God's prophetic word now had respect for and believed the man of God. When I preach, people believe in God's word.

BRINGING UNITY TO THE CHURCH COOPERATION WITH PASTORS

In 1979, the Lord helped me bring many pastors together in unity and prayer. He put on my heart to start a Prayer League of Pastors which meets on the first Monday of every month to pray for the country, for each other and for souls. Because of that God enabled us to have mutual crusades and consequently establishing other pastor's leagues around the country and co-sponsoring open air meetings held with Christian harmony. It was the beginning of working together in pastoral brotherhood.

Now, we are in contact with most of the pastors throughout Haiti. Such ongoing networking results in a leadership conference drawing as many as 2,000 to 4,000 pastors to join together with us.

We attend each other's conventions and churches. This unity is bearing fruit to this day.

God has blessed us with many more miracles. In 1986, when Duvalier left, many who disliked the church or the message we were preaching came to destroy our church but the Lord struck fear into them. Observers saw them running as if being chased, yet no one was running after them. We could tell they were fearful; some of them claiming that they saw a bunch of soldiers giving them chase; maybe angels but no earthly soldiers.

CHAPTER 7

Explosive Growth
A Joyous Burden

The Lord spoke to my heart not to stay in the States, but to come back to Haiti and take care of the ministry. We obeyed His voice and returned to Haiti even though it was a time when we had no home to live in. We believed in God had faith that He would help and sure enough, He provided a place for us. God found us a home at Waney 93, Carrefour. We started a school, in that little house, with just 53 children. The first day 18 children accepted Christ. I started my small church with them and their parents.

Then that little church moved to the porch of our home. God increased our congregation until the porch was inadequate and we decided to add on to the existing house. So, by faith because we had no funds, we began digging a foundation for a new and larger church right in the yard of our home. Eventually with a lot of help from our friends we built a church on that foundation, which now has close to 4,000 members. Today we oversee and coordinate 270 churches and 65 schools. The Lord gave me this strength through His wisdom. The Lord also blessed me with my wife, who is a wonderful helpmate and all the people who support us financially, help us physically and advice us wisely.

I am not in ministry by myself. God has placed many blessed men and women, at my side, who have caught the vision and work with me. I appreciate His help and for all who have become a part of this ministry. Good things are happening because of them.

WALKING IN OUR FAITH

We had to buy the property in front of where our church is now and one morning, we saw the owner who was selling the only parcel of land left. I asked him, "What are they going to do here?" He told me that many were interested in the property and that one wanted to put a night club here. I said, "That cannot be. This land must be sold to my church." He replied, "I knew you had no money to buy it, so I did not offer it to you." I answered, "I want to buy it." He told me he wanted $5,000 for it. At that time, in 1976 that amount was like $500,000 to me, simply because we did not have it. He said, "Okay. I'll give you one week to come up with the money and then I will sell it to you. If not, you cannot have it." That was on a Wednesday.

On Tuesday of the following week, Pastor Luke Weaver, from Grace Chapel Church arrived from Pennsylvania, USA to visit us. He had brought a $500 love gift from his church to bless us with. I told him of our urgent need and the promise I made to buy the land and that I was going to try to use the $500 towards the land. I took Pastor Luke with me to see the land man, on Wednesday morning, exactly one week after my promise. We prayed that he would accept $500.

The man was not happy at all to know that we had only brought him $500 instead of the $5,000 that he wanted. Finally, after much prayer and talk, he accepted the small down-payment. God had moved on the heart of the man to receive our offer and payments were made $10, $20, $50 at a time until our debt was paid off. On this land, we built a school which is also used as a Children's Church, for Youth activities and sometimes for seminars.

Almost everything that we've accomplished has started out with nothing but a vision thus allowing God to open the floodgates of heaven and pour down His blessings on us. This is the principle of faith that God gave me through my father's teaching and it works every time. My father, also built churches by faith with little or no money to begin with.

FACING OPPOSITION

It was not an easy road. We were confronted with many satanic attacks.

The Waney neighborhood was a stronghold for satanic activities. People were afraid to travel on Waneys' streets, even in day time. We had to engage in spiritual warfare, fasting and prayer constantly.

I was a new pastor, only 26 years old and went through many spiritual challenges. Masonic Lodge and Voodoo People tested my spiritual strength frequently. Often times they conspired together and called me to visit a demon possessed home, just to challenge me.

Thank God, the power of the Holy Ghost always prevailed and made us victorious. God always sets the captives free, heals the sick and saves souls.

PASTOR'S OPPOSITION

When our church buildings start getting too small, we kept starting new satellite churches in the nearby localities, with more than 100 people getting saved every month. I became very sick from over working myself.

One afternoon, while I was suffering in bed with a high fever, headaches and vomiting, I was told that a group of pastors had arrived to see me. I was pleased that they came but felt too weak to receive them. So I sent word to tell them that I was sick and could not come out to talk with them.

They insisted to come in to my room and 12 of them entered. Being so sick, I could barely say hello to them. They began angrily admonishing me that their churches were getting empty, they learned that my church was growing too fast and that their members were coming to my church. I replied, "I am not able to discuss this now. Will you, men of God, pray for my healing today and perhaps we can discuss this subject later"? They replied, "No, we're not leaving this room until we get a guarantee from you that you will not take any of our sheep into your disturbing church. I answered their terse ultimatum, "I have not established a membership system in my church and have no way to know who are anyone's sheep or which people are without a congregation".

The fever was so high in me that I implored them, "Would you please allow me to rest"? With anger they retorted, "No, we need a real answer now or we will report you to the Haitian Government as a trouble maker in our city"! I was forced to make a commitment to them that I would only receive new converts with no affiliation from any of their churches in the area.

Placated, they pronounced, "Good, now we're going to pray for you". I begged leave of them, answering, "No, it's o.k., I'll be fine". I thought they were going to pray for my last breath and see me killed; since I felt closer to death than life. They all lifted their voices together and I heard a couple of them saying, "Lord, take care of him right now!" I whispered, "Lord, please not now, I am not ready to die yet, please do not answer their prayer". Thank God, the prayer was very short and they left my room. Most of them became good friends of mine as time passed. No, it's not an easy road. But when God calls you, He makes provision for your success.

OPPOSITION BRINGS PROMOTION PEOPLE CALL ME "SUCCESSFUL"

Am I a success because worldly people call me a millionaire. "No!" I say, "My success is all because of God and what He did for my life; putting me in a position I had never dreamed of achieving. I attribute this blessing first of all to the faithfulness of God, because He said in His Word, that He would raise up the poor out of the dust and would set them on a level with the great men of their period. Some other pastors call me "Big Pastor". Because of God, people look at me as a successful man.

I believe it does not matter where one is born. I was born, in a little village, not in a hospital but in a humble home, in the dark. They had to use candles to see my face and use a razor blade to cut my umbilical cord when I was born. God did not look critically on that most modest beginning and does not want us to focus on our origins. He sets no preconditions to bless us but will do so however we begin our lives journeys. I believe His promise that He would use me; which is exactly what He is doing. I also believe that when you obey God's voice and trust in Him; He will call and you must answer Him.

When I accepted a Bible from my father as "my inheritance"; I believe that God knew I had the faith to just trust Him, work for Him and then be rewarded. I believe the blessing God has given me is attributed to my obedience to Him.

Discover what plan and direction He has for you; follow it and He will bless you with success.

FOLLOWED BY STRANGE DONKEYS

One night, while returning from a mission in the mountains, some donkeys began following our car, keeping up with us no matter how fast we drove.

It was a 6 hour journey and 3 times we were stopped by a flat tire. Looking around we didn't see those donkeys but each time we resumed our trip those strange donkeys appeared again, chasing after us. After 5 hours of being pursued by those animals; I stopped the car. Pretending we had another flat tire. The donkeys were not visible to us. We gathered many stones and resumed driving.

Once more the donkeys pursued us with supernatural speed. We made a sudden stop, got out of the car, and began hurling the stones at our four legged pursuers who turned and fled in such haste they sounded like rushing rivers and stormy winds. Those demon donkeys disappeared for good.

> **"Submit yourselves therefore to God. Resist the devil, and he will flee from you." James 4:7**

CARRIED BY STRANGE HANDS OUT OF THE RIVERBED

Another time, on our way to the mountains to attend our regional convention our truck got stuck in the mud crossing a river bed at Bois-Leger. All the passengers got out pushing and dislodging the wheels from the muck but after many hours of unsuccessfully trying we were at an impasse. A group of about 200 strangers approached the riverbed and for almost an hour they stood there silently observing our dilemma, unresponsive to us. One of them, riding a big white horse, seemed to be their leader.

I approached him and asked, "Are you guys a church group or a community group? Where are you going to, this late at night?" He didn't respond. I continued, "We have been stuck here for several hours, can your group help push our truck out of this river?"

With bowed head he continued to sit silently on his horse. 30 minutes later I repeated the same request with the same mute result.

Suddenly, this odd bunch commenced speaking among themselves in a language that none of us could understand and then became mute again.

After about 15 minutes of mutual silence the leader screamed out to his followers "Pick the truck up out of the riverbed!" Instantly responding in unison the odd bunch came and picked up the truck, with most of us still sitting in it, and lifted its massive weight up and out of the riverbed.

Once out of the river, I started up the vehicle and approached the strange horse mounted leader to thank him. After another 10 minutes of silence, he exclaimed, "Do you know who I am and who got you out of your dilemma today?" I asked, "Are you the Mayor or the police chief?" I am 'Sapirèd'" he roared. "And who is Sapired?" I questioned. He snarled back, "Ask others and you will find out". The entire odd ménage swiftly retreated and disappeared.

We proceeded on to our convention and had a wonderful 3 day God anointed program. On our way back I stopped in the area to inquire of its local people who 'Sapirèd' was. We learned that he was the chief sorcerer in the Region, with alleged powers to kill and to heal.

When it comes to Christians, sorcerer's powers to kill don't work. However God can use anyone to serve His children. Aren't you glad you are a child of the living God?

COOPERATION WITH OTHER PASTORS

We started out alone but soon other Pastors joined us in the work. We had a revival and invited a different church every night resulting in our cooperative efforts. In 1979, the Lord put on my heart to start a Prayer League of Pastors which meets on the first Monday of every month to pray for the country, for each other and for souls. This led to our having crusades together and due to that we are establishing other pastor's leagues around the country. We are in contact with most of the pastors throughout Haiti. Such ongoing networking results in our invitation to a crusade drawing as many as 2,000 to 4,000 pastors to join together with us in the work.

"PAPA" AND "BABY" DOC

Former President Duvalier or "Papa Doc" had lots of respect for Christians. Somebody told him that they heard the Protestant churches were praying too loud, they were growing too large and this resulted in a threat to his government. Papa Doc replied, "If everyone in Haiti was a Protestant Christian, I could walk in the streets without my bodyguards. Nobody would kill me!" He believed that Protestant Christians were non-violent and were not going to try to kill him.

He was, however, terrified of the other groups and people because he knew they could kill him and were more aggressive. He never attacked the Protestant churches; nor did his son, "Baby Doc"; but we were impacted by the urban violence and killings going on. There was a time when some of our Christian brothers were arrested, not because they were Christians, but because somebody told the authorities that they did not like Papa Doc.

There was an incident when a family picture along with one of Papa Doc was found under a pillow in Deacon Rene Orema's home in Dupuy Thiote. He covered them from damage while painting in his house. Everyone was ordered to have Papa Doc's picture hung up on a wall. The Tonton Macoutes (Papa Doc's personal army) came to his house and saw that the picture was down. They arrested him and were going to kill him.

My father heard that Brother Rene was arrested and would be killed. In his record book he noticed that Deacon Rene always paid his tithe to the Lord. My father prayed a prayer of supplication for him and told the Lord please save him or give him all his tithe back. Only by God's intervention was he spared. Papa Doc and his Tonton MaCoutes rained fear on everybody; but there were no direct attacks on the churches.

RESPECT IS PART OF OUR CULTURE

In Haiti, we believe in respect for the authorities and each other. Our government respects us pastors; always referring to us by our titles; as common folk also do. It is a cultural courtesy showing respect for each other. We very rarely call someone by their first name; always his or her title, Mr., Mrs., or Miss. Christians always call each other; brother or sister before their names, like "brother Jack, sister Nancy."

In fact, it is very offensive and disrespectful not address people in this manner; always his or her title first, like Dr. Luke, Bishop Patrick, Pastor Doris, Mrs. or Madam Jeune if married, Miss. (Mademoiselle) Jane. In the church people always call each other Brother or Sister Ed or Kathy.

Children respect their elders and parents, teachers and everyone shows respect to their elders and all authorities.

It is preferable and even advisable to address my wife as Pastor Doris, Madam or Sister Jeune. The same principle applies for all married ladies and women in leadership positions. It is more acceptable to address a Pastor or Bishop as Pastor Bill, Bishop Samson or Brother Isaac instead of calling them by their first name. My wife and I, because of our many years of travel to the United States, are no longer bothered by American informal ways of speech and salutations. However in Haitian terms such casual informality is offensive and disrespectful to us and our Haitian culture.

My wife and I have also gained some respect from non Haitian people who have observed our dedication to God and see that we are not seeking after personal glory but all that we are doing is for God. I think that is why people respect us.

MANY MINISTRIES WITH TOO LITTLE SPACE

The need for more space for our ministries many activities, in serving the Lord and our people, became obvious and urgent. So I dropped on my knees to pray and despite lacking a monetary budget to work with; by faith, I started searching all over Carrefour looking for land to purchase.

I found a 10 acre lot at Lamentin 54 for which the Lord provided start up funds through some supporters like Joyce and Dick Helman, Branch Fellowship and Pennridge Full Gospel that allowed me to make the first down payment.

Soon after that deposit Haiti Love and Faith Ministries paid for one third of the total price. The Christian ladies group and many others in my church made a commitment to get together on the land to pray until the Lord provided the rest of the money to pay it off.

We also organized numerous miracle crusades on the land where many people got saved, healed and delivered. Pastor Mahess Shavda was one of the first Evangelists who had a powerful crusade on our new property.

A financial miracle, to pay off the land, happened in just a few months and I was able to buy more land that was available on the adjacent lot.

Soon after we paid off that next parcel of land, I called on God's army of Love to come and help. Pastor Billy Joe and Sharon Daugherty came to visit and saw the need to begin holding services on this new land so they provided a big Gospel tent with a capacity of 4,000.

David Wine sold us the Tent and put it up for us.

We had some big tent crusades each month that allowed us to start the church in a very short time

We held monthly tent crusades that helped raise funds and facilitated construction on our new church at Lamentin in a very short time. With God's faithfulness and miraculous provision, through His people, we began building the Grace Tabernacle Church.

Pastors Bob Kratz, Bill Moore and Phil Tasker along with teams from the Branch Fellowship, Victory Christian Center, Christ Community Church, Gospel Crusade, Grace Chapel and many others joined together with our church members to construct that church at Lamentin.

Haiti Love and Faith Ministries from Kansas raised funds and built the beautiful girls orphanage home. Teen Missions and Haiti Love partnered with us to build the school that has, for many years; with our wonderful teachers staffing it, been educating thousands of children.

Our home church is Grace Tabernacle located at our Grace Village compound in Carrefour and we are starting up new churches every year along with the many existing ones under our stewardship.

Our second mother church at Grace Village Lamentin

Our Grace Medical and Dental Clinic, also at Lamentin and situated near our Grace Haiti Pediatric Hospital has been serving the community for many years.

Grace Medical & Dental Clinic.
Many patients overflowing the waiting room

We have a Bible School, Victory Bible Institute (VBI), which was started on our Campus by our dear friend Pastor Billy Joe Daugherty, it is now sponsored by Pastor Sharon Daugherty's Victory Christian Institute from Tulsa, Oklahoma. This Bible School has graduated hundreds of students. These graduates are learning how to trust God, preach the Gospel and win people to Christ. Many of them have traveled all over Haiti and started churches and we are joyful about this.

Children's church is a big part of our ministry. We minister to thousands of children through our churches.

One of our Children's Churches

We have many other ministries that God has bestowed upon us; keeping ourselves productively busy for the Master, occupying the land until He comes.

RADIO DAYS

We produce a weekly radio ministry which elicits much favorable response as it broadcasts to the entire island of Haiti and part of the Dominican Republic.

MEDIA ANOTHER WAY TO REACH MY PEOPLE

In 1970, after graduating from Bible Seminary; along with some American missionaries, I produced a radio program on La Voix du peuple AM radio, as well as four other radio stations across Haiti. Later on I had programs on Radio MBC, Caraibe, Cacique, Trans Artibonite, radio Nouvelle and several others. On these broadcasts I taught the bible and preached the Gospel of Jesus Christ for many years.

The 700 Club, on which, in 1985, I shared my testimony with their viewing audience, was my first appearance on television. Later, I was on the Richard Robert's Show. Shortly before these appearances members of my church were having dreams of me preaching on television; an idea that seemed incredible to me at the time.

Following the Richard Robert's Show; brother Schambach, my good friend, supporter and surrogate father figure, introduced me to Paul and Jan Crouch (founders of the Trinity Broadcasting Network). After hearing about what was happening in Haiti they asked me to do a television program for the network to be aired in Haiti and other Haitian Communities around the world.

I had no experience with television and was apprehensive about doing this but they promised to teach and help me in this endeavor. Doris and I were given training and air time at WHFT T.V., TBN's Hollywood, Florida station.

Many television guests testified to millions of viewers how Christ changed their lives

For 21 years from 1985 until 2006 we produced and hosted The Haitian Praise the Lord program which was shown on several stations such as TeleHaiti, Tele PVS, channel 4, Channel 13, Tele Venus in Cap-Haitian, Tele Artibonite and some stations in Miami and South Florida.

This radio and television ministry elicited favorable responses as it broadcasted to the entire island of Haiti and part of the Dominican Republic.

This program has reached and impacted countless influential people on various levels of Haitian society and has educated them about what happened at Bois-Caiman thus aiding the struggle to return our country to God.

We continue to produce a nationally broadcast radio program; also heard in parts of the Dominican Republic. God has opened many doors for us and through the media we've reached innumerable people for Him.

I also travel, ministering in the Caribbean Islands, Central America, North and South America, Africa, Israel, South Korea and Europe; preaching the Gospel and telling people about how God has delivered Haiti from the curse of Voodoo, transforming it into a Christian nation. We have many other ministries that God has bestowed upon us; keeping ourselves productively busy for the Master, occupying the land until He comes. We continue to need God's people to pray for and support us.

FEEDING THE CHILDREN

The first feeding program that we conduct for the children is divided into three sections and three activities. Children in the orphanages are fed three times daily and have a safe, secure room to live in. We provide the education and the love, etc., everything they need to make this a family home for them.

The second feeding program is at our school. The students eat a nutritious lunch which for many of them is the one and only meal they can count on each day.

The third program feeds the street children and all are welcome to partake and participate. Additionally, every summer for three months, six days a week, we include a Bible study for them; learning to worship God and much more.

GREAT SATISFACTION FOR ME

My greatest personal satisfaction is seeing souls coming to Christ; growing up in the knowledge of God, becoming leaders and then training others to bring more souls to Christ. Another of my joys is seeing how many people have become involved in defeating Voodoo.

In 1978, the Voodoo population numbered 80 percent. Now, according to statistics, Voodoo is at 3.11 percent. Praise God! To know that I have had a small part in this is very satisfying. I am glad that I did not leave Haiti when things were very rough but stayed through the tough times. I believe that these spiritual, positive changes are some of the fruits of our suffering. This positive progress brings us great satisfaction.

What we are doing continues bearing fruit. As we keep pressing forward to answer God's call and fulfill his vision, more great changes will happen. More wonderful blessings will take hold in our land.

Our country will be transformed ever more. We look forward to the day when our people are set free from economic bondage, from spiritual and various social problems. I'm not saying it's going to be like heaven, but as our God inspired efforts faithfully prevail, Haiti will be better. The next generation will know better days than what ours has lived through in Haiti.

MY DAILY SCHEDULE

I awake and arise between 5:00 and 6:00 A.M. Roosters crow and dogs bark all night long but one adjusts and sleeps despite the sounds.

At four thirty A.M. the bell rings for all on the grounds to get ready for morning devotion and Bible study at 5:00 A.M. on school days and 6:00 A.M. on weekends and Holidays.

About 5:00 A.M. Carrefour wakes up with its daily exuberance. People singing and the sounds of trucks and cars driving past our compound are my alarm clock.

My very full days usually begin with people calling me at 6:00 A.M. and continuing to call until 11:00 P.M. My appointments commence with people coming to see me by 8:00 A.M.; soon after my devotion which is often cut short by early arrivals. In order to eat my breakfast I have to ignore the ringing telephone.

Numerous meetings occupy my day and just when I think I am finished another group arrives and awaits me.

As busy as my schedule looks, it's nothing as hectic as it was in the beginning. I was practically the wheel that turned everything. I was the one to open and close the church doors, arrange the chairs and pews, set up and control the sound system, lead the worship, play the keyboard instruments, accordion and trumpet, take the offering, make the announcements, preach and pronounce the benediction.

After service I would drive our truck to take our congregation's people home. My wife was responsible for the children's Sunday school, visitor's greetings and maintaining order during the church services.

During the week, Monday through Saturday my wife and I, after taking our kids to school in the morning, worked all day as the office managers and receptionists.

At the same time I was, hands on, constructing our church and school. In the evening, when I didn't have church services, I had meetings with other leaders or a revival service somewhere. I was the one to lead the all night Friday prayer meeting as well as the all day Saturday prayer fast. I just can't figure out how I could have done all that.

TOO BUSY, TOO SICK, TOO TIED UP

Being too burdened and more zealous than wise and not taking better care of our physical bodies often got both my wife and me sick. We have been hospitalized occasionally, despite how much faith we had to stay free of illness.

One time, after being released from the hospital I was still sick and weak but had to get everything prepared for Sunday communion service. On that same weekend, Papa Luke, my Mentor and adopted spiritual father arrived from Pennsylvania, USA to visit and minister to our congregation.

That Sunday morning, I was barely able to stand or do anything but I could not imagine that anything could proceed without my hands on involvement.

The service proceeded for several hours and, still weak from my recent illness, I sat down to rest before getting ready to serve the communion.

Just before I stood up to distribute the communion sacraments, I asked all the people in the congregation to close their eyes and prepare their hearts and spirits for a few minutes of prayer. While my own eyes were closed, I felt hands take hold of me from both sides. When I opened my eyes I saw Papa Luke and some of my leaders tying me down, with a rope, to my chair. I thought it was just a funny joke but I remained tied to my chair until others finished serving communion to the congregation. Initially I was unhappy, for this was the first time in my ministry that I realized I could allow others to conduct ministry functions, albeit under my supervision.

I pray this story will help some younger ministers reading it. Be wise, delegate some functions to others and take care of your physical health.

Once I went up to the mountains with Brother David Gingrich of Canada. He observed that I, being so tired, had reclined in bed to rest; yet was receiving and conversing with a long line of people one after another. I had no idea how long the line was but was told later that it stretched quite a way, outside.

Days can be very busy but I enjoy what God gives me to do. Whatever He asks you to do He gives you the strength to do it and gives you the anointing to accomplish it. If, however, you are not anointed for a task, then don't embark upon it because you will kill yourself. Often the burden seems so heavy but if God is with you, He will give you His strength and His grace to prevail.

SOW THE SEED AND GOD WILL BRING THE HARVEST

> **"Those who sow in tears will reap with songs of joy. He who goes out weeping, carrying seed to sow, will return with songs of joy, carrying sheaves with him." Psalms 126:5,6**

In 1973 while pastoring the little Arcachon church; my wife and I went out, faithfully, twice a week, to go house to house, one on one witnessing. One Saturday morning, we went to a Voodoo temple where more than 20 people had gathered and were playing cards. We started handing Gospel tracts to everyone until we approached the chief Witch Doctor whose name was Monechris. He got very angry when he noticed that all his followers, including his wife, gladly received the Gospel booklets. He started pushing and kicking us out. His wife joined him in throwing rocks at us as we ran out of his house. We thanked God for the opportunity to give them the message and to leave safely.

After two years, we moved away from Arcachon to start a new church in Waney and I lost all contact with the people of

Arcachon. I never knew what happened with Monechris' family or their Voodoo temple.

Ten years later, I was the National Coordinator of a big crusade, for R. W. Schambach, at the Sylvio Cator Soccer Stadium in Port-au-Prince, Haiti. One night during the crusade, as I was walking towards the platform to start the service, a lady stopped me, grabbing my hand and proclaiming, "Do you know who I am?" I looked at her and replied, "No, I don't know who you are and I have no time now to learn who you are. Let me go now. Please try to catch me later."

She asserted, "No! I have to tell you this right now!" I felt disturbed, but since I had no choice, I said, "Okay, tell me quickly, so I can go to start the meeting." "I am Madame Monechris," she said, "Do you remember Monechris?" I answered, "No, who is he? Why is it important for me to know him?"

She reminded me, "Monechris was the powerful Witch Doctor at Arcachon 32. Ten years ago, you and your wife, came to our house and Voodoo temple, to bring us little Gospel booklets. Monechris, my husband, and I threw rocks at you and kicked you out. As you ran through the gate, you told us that God would visit with us soon!"

She continued, "A few years ago, my husband Monechris got very sick and was dying. Our papa Legba (Voodoo Father) could not heal him. I went and got the little Gospel book from under my mattress where I had hidden it, all those years, since you came to our house. I read its' words to Monechris and he prayed to Jesus and became a Christian. I also prayed with him and before he died we both accepted Jesus."

"For more than six years, I have been a faithful church member, and a Deaconess. I go everywhere telling people about Jesus." I exclaimed, "Wow! Thank you so much for sharing this wonderful testimony with me!" That night I called her to come testify before the thousands at the crusade. Many souls came to Christ because of her powerful report!

LET US SOW THE SEED

"Do you not say, 'four months more and then the harvest?'I tell you, open your eyes and look at the fields! They are ripe for harvest." John 4:35

WITNESS TO WITCH DOCTORS

We send out groups to witness to the witch doctors; usually going to the Voodoo temples. Most of the time the beating on the Voodoo drums will stop and the Voodooists will listen to our witness. Even if the Voodooists do not get saved, they are assured that we will be praying for them and that they will in time come to Jesus. Now we have little resistance from the Voodoo people. They accept to be preached to and witnessed to.

CHAPTER 8

Listening To God

God began speaking to me before I went to Bible school. He told me to dedicate my life in service to Him. As I began Bible school my calling was clear.

God tells me all about the future of the church as well as the next plan for our ministry; about the world situation and about my responsibility, as a Christian, for my country. He talks to me about stepping out to help change the history of Haiti also if and when I should accept invitations to other countries. God speaks to my heart; sometimes through prophecies that I consider to see how they line up with His Word.

For many years, I was closed to receiving from God but now, through experience, I can recognize His voice much better and have more discernment about how to comprehend His message. He speaks to me about using His wisdom in transmitting His message in a way that people can understand, so it can be more effective toward achieving God's will.

Hearing from God requires abundant prayer and fasting. We fast and spend an entire day, with God, once every month. My wife also does, one day, every week. The first Friday of the month she fasts from 6 a.m. to 6 p.m. whenever I travel, I try to take time to be alone with God.

I have always had a close relationship with Jesus since, at 12 years old, I accepted Him into my life. I have never been sorry for walking with Jesus, for He touched and changed my life. This is what has sustained me through all my hard times because I realized that He is more than a natural father to me. I've experienced God's fatherly love through Jesus.

There were many times when my father, because of his frequent trips, was gone. I needed someone like a father but I see that Jesus has been that to me. He has been my protector, my counselor, my doctor, my best friend, my helper and constant provider. He is everything to me.

I have a special relationship with Him and when I call on Him for what I do not have or what I need to be, He meets me where I am and fulfills the desires of my heart. He gives me what I need to have and brings me strength and joy when I am empty.

CONSTANT SEARCH FOR HIS WISDOM

Many times I make mistakes. In the natural, my wife is more sensitive to me than I am to myself. She has better intuition about people and situations. Discerning, there will be a problem in dealing with something or somebody; she will usually say, "This is not right. This man is not telling you the truth." I will reply, "No, leave him alone." I discover later that she is usually right. Many times I am wrong. I don't always get right to the point. Sometimes I miss the mark and when we are faced with big decisions we have to earnestly pray to find God's will and His thinking to successfully resolve the challenge confronting us.

There are times when we make mistakes, but through prayer and the Holy Ghost, God guides our decisions. We must depend on Him and not try to solve every situation alike.

I rely on my personal relationship with the Lord and seek constantly to strengthen it. I need to read my Bible and pray more. I need to spend more time alone with the Lord. My wife is more faithful, than I am, in spending time alone with the Lord. I need to make an effort to seek God's face more than I do now.

GOD SPEAKS IN THE SHOWER

God talks to me in the shower. I believe it is because I spend more time, by myself, in the shower, than any other place: so God has uninterrupted time to talk to me. Taking a shower is where I got the revelation about overthrowing the kingdom of Satan by breaking the Voodoo curse over Haiti.

Every moment I'm led in different ways by God who always gives me the right direction. The Lord uses many things and different people to help us make the right decisions.

I try to hear from God every day. I want to hear God's voice more distinctly to be sure of what He is trying to tell me; especially if there is danger and risk, to people's lives, involved.

POSITIVE CONFESSION FOR AN END TO VIOLENCE

A leader's vision is always positive. He sees a better tomorrow. When I see tires burning in the street, I know this is the work of the devil. This gives me a reason to pray more and to thank God for the new Haiti. The new Haiti will be under the leadership of God, administered by Godly Christians; who will show the difference between the current chaos and what He can do. When I see violence in action, I tell people to get their cameras and take pictures as evidence of it, to help show the difference between a country under the leadership of God and one under the control of Satan. There is a positive way to look at difficult situations.

STILL HUMAN

Many times I get discouraged but have always preached not to expose your discouragement. Don't let it be published in the media, so as not to diminish your standing as a leader. First, pray or fast; then turn to other leaders who are involved with the same or similar battles and who will understand what you're going through.

We were faced with an attack on our property and the church in Lamentin. Some gangs were trying to invade our property; they were mad at us. I told them that we have always trusted in God and He is our strength.

At one time, a group of young men arrived at my office and told me they were going to shoot up my house and that I had to leave the country immediately. I felt concerned when they told me that. Suddenly, God's power came over me and the Holy Spirit said, through His scripture, "You are not your own. You belong to Him. Your body and yourself are not your own." I answered my assailants, "When is all this going to happen?" They said it would happen very soon. (This was at a time when Aristide was trying to return to power after being ousted from Haiti.) I replied, "I am not leaving. I belong to God. I am His property. He will not let me be destroyed by gangs. I am not going anywhere."

The young men then said, "Bishop, this is very serious." They did not want me to get hurt and had plane tickets for us to depart with. I answered, "If God cannot protect me, then let me be killed!" The power of God came over me and I rebuked them. A few days later most of the gang members were killed in a fight between their own mob and the police. God always helps us in our hours of need.

Some great disappointments have beset our ministry; promises of help which engendered hope that God was going to change the Haitian situation soon. When the president began to call in Voodoo spirits, all of the Christians said, "NO." It seemed like the demons were winning a victory over prayer. That caused some discouragement.

God has sent us the message about Moses and the Children of Israel coming out of Egypt. I realize how long it took; and how Moses was very, very disappointed when he went to Pharaoh and told him about God and wanted to send the children out of Egypt. Instead of things getting better, things got worse.

The children of Israel told Moses, "God is going to judge you because we were living here. It was hard for us already. 'No,' you make it even harder for us. Then the Lord will judge you." Moses was so disappointed; he went to the Lord and said, "Lord, why did you send me?"

"Now the people are having more trouble than they had before. You told me You were going to deliver them and take them out. You did not deliver them at all. You embarrassed me. You disappointed me."

> **1 "And afterward Moses and Aaron went in, and told Pharaoh, Thus saith the Lord God of Israel, Let my people go, that they may hold a feast unto me in the wilderness.**
>
> **2 And Pharaoh said, Who is the Lord, that I should obey his voice to let Israel go? I know not the Lord, neither will I let Israel go.**
>
> **3 And they said, The God of the Hebrews hath met with us: let us go, we pray thee, three days' journey into the desert, and sacrifice unto the Lord our God; lest he fall upon us with pestilence, or with the sword.**
>
> **4 And the king of Egypt said unto them, Wherefore do ye, Moses and Aaron, let the people from their works? Get you unto your burdens.**
>
> **5 And Pharaoh said, Behold, the people of the land now are many, and ye make them rest from their burdens.**
>
> **6 And Pharaoh commanded the same day the taskmasters of the people, and their officers, saying,**
>
> **7 Ye shall no more give the people straw to make brick, as heretofore: let them go and gather straw for themselves.**

8 And the tale of the bricks, which they did make heretofore, ye shall lay upon them; ye shall not diminish ought thereof: for they be idle; therefore they cry, saying, Let us go and sacrifice to our God.

9 Let there more work be laid upon the men, that they may labour therein; and let them not regard vain words.

10 And the taskmasters of the people went out, and their officers, and they spake to the people, saying, Thus saith Pharaoh, I will not give you straw.

11 Go ye, get you straw where ye can find it: yet not ought of your work shall be diminished.

12 So the people were scattered abroad throughout all the land of Egypt to gather stubble instead of straw.

13 And the taskmasters hasted them, saying, Fulfill your works, your daily tasks, as when there was straw.

14 And the officers of the children of Israel, which Pharaoh's taskmasters had set over them, were beaten, and demanded, Wherefore have ye not fulfilled your task in making brick both yesterday and today, as heretofore?

15 Then the officers of the children of Israel came and cried unto Pharaoh, saying, Wherefore dealest thou thus with thy servants?

16 There is no straw given unto thy servants, and they say to us, Make brick: and, behold, thy servants are beaten; but the fault is in thine own people.

17 But he said, Ye are idle, ye are idle: therefore ye say, Let us go and do sacrifice to the Lord.

18 Go therefore now, and work; for there shall no straw be given you, yet shall ye deliver the tale of bricks

19 And the officers of the children of Israel did see that they were in evil case, after it was said, Ye shall not minish ought from your bricks of your daily task.

20 And they met Moses and Aaron, who stood in the way, as they came forth from Pharaoh:

21 And they said unto them, The Lord look upon you, and judge; because ye have made our labor to be abhorred in the eyes of Pharaoh, and in the eyes of his servants, to put a sword in their hand to slay us.

22 And Moses returned unto the LORD, and said, Lord, wherefore hast thou so evil entreated this people? Why is it that thou hast sent me?

23 For since I came to Pharaoh to speak in thy name, he hath done evil to this people; neither hast thou delivered thy people at all." Exodus 5:1-23

Then the Lord told him that he had hardened the heart of Pharaoh. He is going to create a miracle to get His children out. Like the Israelites, we are very courageous and have faith that God is going to change the situation.

THANK YOU JESUS FOR RENEWED YOUTH !

Hallelujah! **They that wait upon the Lord, shall renew their strength! They shall mount up with wings as**

Eagles; they shall run, and not be weary; they shall walk, and not faint. Isaiah 40:31

15) My substance was not hid from thee, when I was made in secret, and curiously wrought in the lowest parts of the earth.

16) Thine eyes did see my substance, yet being unperfect; and in thy book all my numbers were written, which in continuance were fashioned, when as yet there was none of them.

17) How precious also are thy thoughts unto me, O God! How great is the sum of them!

18) If I should count them, they are more in number than the sand: when I awake, I am with thee. Psalm 139:15-18

CHAPTER 9

The Fall Of Voodoo
Breaking The Back Of Satan

For this purpose the Son of God was manifested, that he might destroy the works of the devil. 1 John 3:8

You are of God, little children, and have overcome them; because greater is He that is in you, than he that is in the world. 1 John 4:4

I believe; a prophesy, regarding my life, that my dad received from God, prior to my birth, foretold the liberation of Haiti through Jesus Christ. God told my Dad in the prophecy "he will be a son and he will do a great, amazing work in the country of Haiti." I believe my spiritual warfare in Bois-Caïman will break the pact made with Satan over Haiti and our taking the land back to God is part of the realization of that prophecy.

We children learned of Catholicism, Voodoo and the Evangelicals at an early age and understanding their differences hated Voodoo and the Devil.

THE NATIVE PEOPLE OF HAITI BEFORE THE AFRICAN SLAVES CAME TO THE ISLAND

When Columbus discovered the island on December 5, 1492, he named it La Isla Island Espanola (Hispaniola), or Spanish Island because of its resemblance to the lands of Castile.

The Taino Amerindians (whose population was estimated at 8 million) were the native peoples. The Spanish, preoccupied with finding Gold, who didn't understand the native language and customs, thought them inferior and slaughtered or enslaved the population. Most of them died as a result of the cruel treatment, forced labor, ethnic executions and European diseases afflicted upon them by the Spanish.

Within 20 years fewer than 28,000 remained alive and by 1542 only 200 had survived this Caribbean Holocaust. Within 50 years of Columbus's arrival the Tainos and their ancient egalitarian culture had all but disappeared.

The name 'Haiti' is an Indian word which means mountains. Two-thirds of all Haiti is mountainous land.

After the Tainos were for the most part dead and gone, the slave masters needed workers to replace them. They made deals with a Catholic Bishop from Portugal to go to Africa and start a slave market to bring workers to the Caribbean Islands. Most Haitians were kidnapped from Senegal, Ghana, Ivory Coast, Guinea and some from Nigeria. Later, the French conquered the Island from the Spanish and became the new slave masters.

Once the African slaves arrived in Haiti, they were sold to their various French masters and committed to lives at forced labor. Being taught that their masters represented God in Heaven and that they represented the Devil; they had to blindly submit to their masters in order to receive forgiveness from their owner's God.

When the slaves came from Africa in the 1600s they experienced many years of suffering. Their treatment was so bad that they cried out for freedom from the curse of many years. Finally they revolted; turning to their Voodoo gods from Africa whom they worshiped now through a mixture of Voodoo and Catholicism.

As the slaves arrived from Africa, they were given pictures of Catholic Saints to worship and required to be baptized into the Catholic Church within eight days. The Black Code of the Slaves published in 1600 provided penalties for all slave masters who did not comply with these requirements. Their land and possessions would be taken away from them leaving them with no right to own slaves again.

They were brought to church every Sunday and worshipped the effigies of the Saints in the same spirit as they had the Voodoo gods in Africa. This mixture of Voodoo and Catholicism is known as Syncretism. They were allowed to have Voodoo ceremonies; taking a picture of the Virgin Mary and calling it "Erzilie Freda" and renaming St. Peter "Ogou Feray".

HAITI WAS DEDICATED TO SATAN

There is an unbridled quest for freedom, which lives in the heart of every living creature. However many of the slaves reverted to their African Voodoo gods; in a misplaced attempt to be free. So it was that they dedicated the country to Satan. The following section of history will help to explain what happened.

BOIS-CAIMAN

The Voodooist slaves were seduced by a lady Witch Doctor called Iman who organized a Voodoo ceremony in the forest where she lived; afterward named Bois-Caiman (Iman's forest).

They sacrificed a pig at this gathering, drank its blood and shed some of it on the ground in a ritual dedication of the land of Haiti to Satan. The ceremonial participants performed a kind of communion to bond together and fight for freedom but unwittingly had communed with the Devil. They declared, "If you give us freedom, we will serve you Papa Legba, (Father Satan), all of our lives. Haiti will be yours forever!"

BOUKMAN'S PRAYER TO GOD IN HEAVEN

Boukman, the great revolutionary from Jamaica who was attending the ceremony prayed to God in Heaven: "Oh God in Heaven; you created the sea, the stars, the moon and all the earth. You hide above the clouds and watch us suffering. We cry to you for freedom! Listen to our cry, come set us free." He commanded the ritualists: "Throw away all your foreign gods." The celebrant slaves witnessed; lightning and thunder, though it wasn't raining. A great fear of this God to whom Boukman was praying settled over them.

He ordered the slaves to get rid of all their foreign gods (images of the Catholic saints and statues given to them) that they had in their hands.

I personally believe that if Boukman or someone else had in the beginning explained how to meet this God in Heaven whom they were calling upon and if they had known that it was through Jesus Christ; receiving Him as Savior at that time, Haiti would have become a Christian nation from its foundation.

Unfortunately, they were informed by the Catholic Saints iconography, which of itself had no unholy implications but when interpolated with their African Voodoo practices cast such as Mary, St. Peter etc., as satanic idols. I also believe that when Boukman told them to cast away their foreign gods and false idols; he was referring to these icons the slaves were encouraged to worship. In fact, no Voodoo gods were alluded to in that prayer; rather a rejection of them. From the foundation of our nation, some of our founding fathers invited God in Heaven while they rejected Voodoo.

WAS BOUKMAN A WITCH DOCTOR OR A BIBLE BELIEVER?

We can say, with reasonable certainty that Boukman seems to have been a Bible believer and not a Voodoo worshipper or Witch Doctor. Iman was the Voodoo Priestess at whose home the ceremony was held. Boukman's role, in that, was to mobilize the crowd of slaves for revolution and before he even started, he prayed to God in heaven in whom he believed.

In general, all believers pray to the god of their religion. When a Muslim prays he speaks to Allah. When a Buddhist prays he does so to Buddha. When a Catholic prays he often does to the Virgin Mary or one of his religions pantheon of saints.

When a Voodoo man prays he does so to Papa Legba, Mèt (Master) Loko and Ogou Feray. When an Evangelical Bible believer prays he will always talk to God in Heaven in the Name of Jesus. Boukman prayed to God in Heaven and thus rejected Voodoo.

It is generally believed that Boukman was a Protestant (Baptist) bible believer from Jamaica who had one arm. He always carried under his arm a little book which many historians believe was a bible that he read daily. That's why people called him the book man that became his real name Boukman. It is very important to understand why Boukman, being from Jamaica, was a Protestant and not a Voodoo worshiper.

All the British islands were of Protestant background while all the French and Spanish islands were Catholic. In the French and Spanish islands the syncretism (a mixture of religious figures with ethnic gods and rituals) is a reality. This might explain why Haiti in so much more mixed up in Voodoo than all the other islands. We were a French colony. The Bahamas and the other British colonized islands were not deeply engaged in Voodoo and Witch Craft, perhaps because they were of Protestant background.

Some Haitian historians and Voodoo supporters believe and argue that God participated and gave His approval to Voodoo practices, because of lightning and thunder attributed to Him. We Christians believe and declare that God is the Father of love; always listening to his children's cries whenever they call upon Him for help. I believe that the lightning and thunder were a signal from the God of heaven after Boukman prayed indicated that help was on the way.

Many Haitian presidents that have come to power in Haiti, whether by election or by coup d'état (overthrow of government) believe they have to go to Bois-Caiman to worship the devil and receive power. Most of them and all the important governmental ministers, have been going to Bois-Caiman each year on August 13th to 14th to worship the devil in celebration of that date and to find power. This is also the reason why the pig has become a Voodoo symbol of worship and Bois-Caiman its most sacred place in Haiti. Most Haitians have always believed that Haiti's independence from France and Spain was won due to the pig's sacrifice at Bois-Caiman.

Voodoo also has strongholds in Miami, Florida, New Orleans, Louisiana and in many other Haitian communities in the United States.

THE REVOLUTION

That first big Bois-Caïman congress had two fold purposes: spiritual/ religious and political/ revolutionary.

In their search for freedom, some of the slaves believed that worshiping the god called Legba and making a pact with him as a superior god and master of Africa would give them favor and strategy in their struggle for freedom. The slaves were allowed by their masters to periodically practice their African rituals. This was, to them, a source of comfort and strength as they socialized and communed with each other.

REVOLUTIONARY PURPOSE

Since the religious gathering was the only meeting occasion permitted to the slaves, Boukman as well as many other non-voodooists took advantage of these gatherings to initiate a revolutionary campaign and start a general revolt for independence. At the end of all the religious and political speeches little stones were given to each slave and they were told to throw away one stone every morning. The day before the last stone that was to be thrown everyone was told to gather together for battle.

Two years after the onset of the French Revolution the enslaved and oppressed people of Haiti revolted from their long bondage under Spain and France.

Commencing in August of 1791, under the leadership of the great Revolutionaries, Boukman, from Jamaica, Makandal from Trinidad and Henri Christophe from Grenada, the slave liberation movement in the Americas was set in motion.

Slave armies, led by Toussaint Louverture and Jean-Jacques Dessalines, both ex-slaves but experienced military generals from Africa, though greatly outnumbered, defeated a combined force of more than 60,000 Spanish and French soldiers.

Eight days following the Bois-Caïman religious and revolutionary congress, on the nights of August 13-14, 1791, the first revolt began all over the island. On August 22, 1791 Boukman, along with many other slaves was executed but the revolution once set in motion could not be stopped, continuing for 13 years and with a final victory of Haiti's freedom from slavery, led to the proclamation of Haiti's independence. On January 1st, 1804, Haiti became the first independent black Republic in the world.

To achieve that freedom and independence many titanic battles were fought with the powerful Napoleonic French army. The French were depleted somewhat by the defection from their ranks of some of their Polish conscripts who, drafted from a Poland which had often been beset by conquering and colonizing neighboring nations, understood the Haitians aspirations for freedom, and joined their righteous cause. The Poles, who were considered to be some of the best warriors in Europe and stopped the invasion of Europe by Islamic armies at Vienna, Austria, fought and died side by side with their adopted Haitian brothers in arms.

Many of those brave Poles, who survived, (most of them died of yellow fever) remained in Haiti, married with Haitians and their descendants still live in a liberated land.

The Independence of Haiti was an inspiration to many other countries and with the struggles for their own independence. Haitians soldiers helped Columbia, Venezuela and also fought with Abraham Lincoln's Northern forces against the South in the American Civil War (notably at the battle of Savannah, Georgia}.

The Louisiana Purchase, which at the time, doubled the size of the United States, was a result of Napoleon, with his occupying forces being defeated, pulling out of Haiti; which was the French garrison in the Caribbean and so close to America and his ambitions there.

Thomas Jefferson's administration paid France a pittance for the millions of square miles but later showed little gratitude to the Haitians who drove French ambitions out of America.

However, to enslaved and colonized peoples in America and elsewhere in the world the Haitian people's revolution was an inspiration for freedom and independence movements of their own.

THE POWER OF PRAYER

Thanks to the power of the Gospel, a new light is shining into the hearts of people causing them to reject these Voodoo beliefs and to accept the truth of the Bible; that freedom comes only through Jesus-Christ.

> **"If the Son therefore shall set you free, you shall be free indeed." John 8:36**

We know the Devil had cast a curse upon the land but as we Christians pray, seek God, and help Him get people saved; He has begun creating a new nation. Christians in Haiti, foreign missionaries residing there and intercessors around the world have continued praying and interceding for Haiti's transformation unceasingly for many years.

In 1977, with an extensive association of pastors and Christian leaders, I founded a prayer league called "La Ligue Fraternelle de Prière" to pray for deliverance from Satan and transformative change in Haiti. Pastors and leaders gather together the first Monday of every month to pray and read the Word of God. Forty day prayer fasts are held every year all over the country led by our Grace Tabernacle Churches, the Church of God, the Prayer Mountain of Sister Marie, Sister Mireille Simon, Prayer Center of Pastor Eddy Francois and many other Christian groups and organizations which intercede, pray and organize crusades and National days of prayer for Haiti.

Several times we held crusades in cooperation with other organizations like CEEH (Concile des Eglises Evangeliques d Haiti), ASHRAM d'Haiti, CONAMISE, CONASPE, Association Des Femmes Ferventes, (End Time Handmaidens and Servants), AFCA, Servantes en Mission, Federation Protestante D'Haiti, Gospel Crusade Of Haiti, Soldats De Christ of Frere Jean-Claude Oscar, Temoins De Christ of Pastor Eddy St.Ange Volcy, Les Combatants of Frere Daniel and Samuel Jn. Baptiste, Centre de priere of Pastor Eddy Francois, ALEGH of Gonaives, ALENH of Cap-Haitian, Ministres Internationaux of Bishop Octamoliere, Vision Haiti of Pastor Gerald and Evangelist Paul Clerie, Genesis Centre de Reveil of Pastor Alexis.

> **If my people, which are called by my name, shall humble themselves, and pray, and seek my face, and turn from their wicked ways; then will I hear from heaven, and will forgive their sin, and will heal their land."**
> **II Chronicles 7:14**

GOD SAID: ENOUGH IS ENOUGH BREAK THE POWER OF THE PIG SPIRIT!

Something special and historical happened in October of 1996. We were holding a miracle crusade, with Pastor Billy Joe Daugherty, from Tulsa, Oklahoma, at the soccer stadium in Carrefour, Haiti. People were getting saved; healings and miracles were taking place every night.

On the final night of the crusade while in the shower preparing for the crusade, God told me quite clearly to break the power of the pig spirit. The pig image recurred over and over in my vision for more than 30 minutes as I showered and I heard God's voice thunder to me, "Break the spirit of the pig over the nation!" I suddenly understood, that God was telling me about the pig which was sacrificed in Bois-Caiman to dedicate the land of Haiti to Satan over 200 years ago.

I rushed to the crusade and gathered all the pastors who were there and very excitedly shared with them the great assignment God gave me to destroy the power of the pig spirit over the nation. I told them, "Let us do something great tonight, something historical to break the satanic power over Haiti." Some pastors said it was not a good idea to bother the Devil and cause the government to persecute Christians.

After extensive discussions with the attending pastors, some were willing to accept my plan and joined me. I called the young people and explained to them what the Lord was showing me. They got the message quickly and ran with it. That spontaneous enthusiasm, they possess, is one reason why I love the youth so much. Chief Fenel Jean-Baptiste led the Boys and Girls Scouts, Chief Chimène Jacques, Viviane Sanon, Nicole Séide, Beleck Pierre and others organized the Brigades and Lights team and other young people in the Church, to create a drama together. They dramatized the story, beginning with the first arrivals, in bondage from Africa through, the years of slavery, to the time when the infamous Voodoo ceremony, in Bois-Caiman, to dedicate Haiti to Satan was conducted.

Those young people painted a big ugly pig on a piece of hardboard to represent the pig that was sacrificed. At the conclusion of this very moving drama, the pastors come on the scene to show how the Gospel can bring true freedom, cast out the darkness and give life to the nation.

We read a Declaration of Spiritual Independence unto Haiti and revoked the pact that our ancestors had made with Satan 200 years ago. Then we publicly burned the pig and raised Haiti's flag toward heaven dedicating it to God; proclaiming that the blue in the flag represents heaven and the red represents the blood of Jesus over Haiti. We took communion together before concluding this great, spiritual and historic event.

In dedicating our country and flag to God, more than 65,000 people who were attending the crusade prayed and cried out to God. The PVS Television channel and many radio stations carried a live broadcast of this crusade to the entire country. We requested the television and radio audience to join us in the dedication prayer and believed there were millions of Christians praying with us.

The government officials saw what we did that night and we heard they were very unhappy. They said that we had betrayed our ancestors' holy culture but, Praise God, we were not persecuted for this action. Nationwide, Christians were encouraged to speak out boldly against the works of witchcraft. We were so happy to have participated in this spiritual accomplishment for our country.

However, God had a bigger assignment at Bois-Caiman, the ground zero location where the Voodoo sacrifice took place 200 years ago!

CONQUEST OF BOIS-CAIMAN FOR JESUS TAKING BACK THE LAND FOR GOD!

God started talking to me about going to conquer Bois-Caiman for Jesus, to break the satanic pact, and to take Haiti back for Him! We thought we had already accomplished that, for Him, in Port-au-Prince, at Carrefour soccer stadium, on behalf of the whole country. There seemed to be no reason or need to travel seven hours to Bois-Caiman to conduct another warfare Crusade. However, the Lord insisted: "Go to the exact location in Bois-Caiman, where the devil was celebrated and consecrated in the first place. The location they call the devil's territory!" I didn't know where it was located. Christians were not allowed to set foot in that place, anyway. It was reserved for Voodoo priests and government officials.

Many people came to tell me about Bois-Caiman: Miss Clernicia, Frère Jodel Gédeus, Frère Jehu Loute, Frère Damas Morency and others told me where it was, how to get there and invited me to go and see it with them.

I had visited other Voodoo sites previously, such as Soukri Danache and Nan Souvenance in the Gonaives area but had never been to Bois-Caiman; which is located 7 km from Cap-Haitian which itself is 7 hours drive (about 175 miles) from Port-au-Prince.

How should I start this daunting and difficult assignment? First, I organized some Pastor's breakfasts to share what God was asking us to do. Few agreed to pray with me about this venture. One pastor stood up at one of our meetings and challenged me, "Bishop Jeune, let me ask you a question. Why do you want to go all the way up to Bois-Caiman and disturb the devil? Why don't you wait for him to come to you and then cast him out? You have a big church in Port-au-Prince, many schools and lots of great ministries, why are you not satisfied with all that God has given you? Why do you want to cause trouble for the devil and create persecutions against the Christians by going to Bois-Caiman?" I thought he had made a good point because in the natural, I didn't really want to go there but my answer was that God was insisting for us to go and I declared, "Whatever the cost may be, we must go!"

MOBILIZATION FOR BATTLE ON BOIS-CAIMAN GROUND

I organized many pastors and leaders meetings; networking with churches throughout Haiti, informing them about God's assignments and suggesting how they might participate.

The spiritual battle plan was to be a coordinated, cooperative Nationwide Day of Prayer; based on complete unity. At the same hour, on that day, we would all simultaneously pray the identical prayer aimed at delivering Haiti from all the Voodoo Spirits and their satanic strongholds.

We continued preparing for the liberation day by placing big signs in front of the Presidential Palace, the Government Office buildings and all the public places; informing the nation that the Satanic pact at Bois-Caiman was going to be broken; that infamous location as well as all of Haiti was going to be conquered for and dedicated to Christ! I wrote official letters notifying all the Governmental Departments of our intentions but received no reply! No news, good news! No reply, good reply!

MOBILIZATION IN MIAMI AND OTHER PARTS OF THE WORLD

Through a television show in Miami, I had the privilege to meet Pastor Gerald and Evangelist Paul Clerie of 'Vision Haiti' who had the same vision to do warfare in Bois-Caiman and take Haiti back for God. I was so excited and consequently partnered with them to create the mobilization in Miami and other communities around the world. The plan was that we all join together in the battle at the same time everywhere in the world.

We mobilized our church and Christians in all the other churches by radio, flyers and letters. Churches all over Haiti were prepared to organize local rallies simultaneously with us while we were engaged in the battle at Bois-Caïman. Only 150 brave soldiers of the cross, traveled with me to Bois-Caiman. The End Time Hand Maidens and Servants of Haiti Branch led by my wife were the intercessors.

Most of the time, the Lord prefers to use a small numbers, rather than a multitude to win a great battle. However, sometimes the participation of many, helps win the battles and blesses all who join forces, far and wide, to grow stronger in their faith due to the experience of a shared effort.

> **2 And the Lord said unto Gideon, the people that are with thee are too many for me to give the Midianites into their hands, lest**
>
> **Israel vaunt themselves against me, saying, mine own hand hath saved me.**
>
> **3 Now therefore go to proclaim in the ears of the people, saying whosoever is fearful and afraid, let him return and depart early from**
>
> **Mount Gilead. And there returned of the people twenty and two thousand; and there remained ten thousand.**
>
> **4 And the lord said unto Gideon, The people are yet too many; bring them down unto the water, and I will try them for thee there; and it shall be, that of whom I say unto thee,**

This shall go with thee, the same shall go with thee; and of whomsoever I say unto thee,

This shall not go with thee the same shall not go.

5 So he brought down the people unto the water; and the Lord said unto Gideon, Every one that lappeth of the water with his tongue, as a dog lappeth, him shalt thou set by himself; likewise every one that boweth down upon his knees to drink.

6 And the number of them that lapped, putting their hand to their mouth, were three hundred men; but all the rest of the people bowed down upon their knees to drink water.

7 And the lord said unto Gideon, By the three hundred men that lapped will I save you, and deliver the midianites into thine hand; and let all the other people go every man unto his place. —Judges 7:2-7

BOIS-CAIMAN SATANIC PACT IS BROKEN! HAITI IS TAKEN BACK FOR GOD

August the thirteenth, is the month and day when the pig sacrifice took place in 1791 and the same day, each year, when the witch doctors and government officials gather together at Bois-Caiman to commemorate that infamous event and stage a Voodoo Celebration.

We announced on the newscasts our intention to be there that day also. One hundred and fifty Christian warriors, who had registered to join the effort, gathered together very early the morning of August the thirteenth, 1997, at my church at Waney 93, Carrefour for the trip to Bois-Caiman.

We boarded the rented buses for our seven-hour journey but first we stopped at the National Palace and led a spiritual warfare prayer effort before leaving Port Au Prince. Gathering around a statue of an upraised hand (named "Maron Inconnu") out of which one of those eternal flames burns; we commenced our day of battles with all the demon spirits. Because many Voodoo sacrifices had been held at the National Palace, it was a good location to begin our attacks against the Devil.

In 1991, the Haitian president held a Voodoo Ritual inside the Haitian Palace. Many prominent government officials and well known witch doctors attended this abomination, drinking potions of fire and rolling around on a mud covered floor. Their unholy purpose was to renew the dedication of Haiti to Satan and reinforce his stronghold within our national seat of government.

After our action at the Palace we traveled all day arriving at Bois-Caiman at eight P.M. to a big surprise! No Voodoo Celebration would take place nor would witch doctors or government officials be there as usual from August thirteen to fourteenth. Those who had gathered and a few Christians from the area were waiting, with great curiosity, to see what was going to happen.

Our original plan was to position ourselves several hundred feet from the demonic celebration site to pray against the activities. "What happened?", we asked. For 200 years the witch doctors had gathered at this site annually on August the 13th; why weren't they present today? Some people replied that when the witch doctors heard the broadcast announcing that Christians were going to invade the Voodoo site, they cancelled their celebration for fear of a confrontation.

I told the onlookers, "We have not come here for a flesh and blood, physical confrontation." We were there for a spiritual battle and heavy duty confrontation with Satan, who had occupied our Father's land for more than 200 years. We came to cancel all contracts and pacts our forefathers had made with demons. I commanded my troops to start marching, singing, shouting, praying and praising God as we invaded that infamous Voodoo site.

Bois-Caiman for Jesus Sign

The Christian Army invaded the Voodoo site

We were told it was the first time Christians had ever come to that site for religious purpose. Before us stood a huge tree, whose trunk was many feet in diameter; which we were told had been there since the first Voodoo sacrifice. Many blood sacrifices had been done under that tree. The Voodoo worshipers, under the influence of demon spirits, would climb up that tree without holding on to it. They would eat pieces of glass bottles, cut themselves and drink the blood and then would shape shift themselves into snakes or other animals. They would put fire in their mouth without being burned.

Converging towards the Voodoo Tree, it felt like we were walking on sand and that a force was pushing us back. Singing and shouting louder; we commanded the demons to fall in submission to the Holy Spirit and pressed on till we reached and encircled the tree. A heaviness in the air was so strong, that we found it difficult to raise our hands up to praise God.

I asked the people to prepare for a Jericho march but before we began I challenged the devil declaring, "Devil, if you have the right to be here, prove it right now! Our ancestors didn't know this Jesus whom we love and serve today. They made a pact with you over our land. We come, as legitimate sons, daughters and heirs of our fathers, to cancel that old pact. I give you five minutes to come up with any deeds or papers that give you the right to inhabit this property."

Five minutes having elapsed, we began our triumphal Jericho March. Seven times, like Joshua of old, we encircled the demon infested tree. Suddenly, like an explosion, emanating from the tree, Sister Henry Merius saw a half human, half animal creature flying out. At this moment all the heaviness was lifted off of us and we all freely lifted our hands in praises to God and continued to worship, sing and dance.

Encouraged, by this change, I continued to cast out all 151 demon spirits by name and commanding them, in the name of Jesus, to be gone from Bois-Caiman, and never to return. I read the Act of Spiritual Independence of Haiti and declared the Satanic Pact canceled in Jesus' name; declaring the curse that was over Haiti to be broken.

We served communion under the Voodoo Tree replacing the blood of the pig with the precious blood of the Lamb, Jesus Christ. Remaining on the site, we held revival crusades for three days during which many people were delivered from the dominion of Voodoo unto the kingdom of Jesus Christ. We established a fellowship with Pastor Pierre Vital for the new converts to be nourished by the word of God, in his little church.

Simultaneous spiritual battles were waged in other parts of Haiti. Pastors rallied Christians from their regions; into soccer stadiums, public places, open fields, churches and to all the highways and byways to pray in unity with us.

SIMULTANEOUS ACTION IN MIAMI WITH VISION HAITI

While we were fighting the battle of Bois-Caiman, Vision Haiti was conducting a warfare crusade at the same time in a soccer stadium in Miami; attended by thousands of Haitian and other nationalities. They also read the Spiritual Independence Act and declared the satanic pact over Haiti broken and canceled, on behalf of all Haitians around the world.

CHIEF WITCH DOCTORS BOW AND KNEEL DOWN

Early on the morning of August the 14th we started looking for the witch doctors to tell them what happened in Bois-Caiman the night before. Pastor Eddy Volcy, my faithful, dynamic Joshua and I went to Cap-Haitian to the Catholic Cathedral where we were told the witch doctors were hiding.

Inside several hundred of the Voodooists were chanting, dancing and beating their drums. We expected some resistance but as soon as they saw us come in, the chief asked that all the noise and movement should stop and he approached us followed by many of his lieutenants; then bowed and knelt down at our feet as they called me "President." I was so shocked; I didn't know what to do. I took them by the hand and asked them to get up. I knew I should pray for them, lead them in the sinner's prayer and hit them on their heads with my Bible. Instead I did nothing but get them up and relate what had happened in Bois-Caiman.

Afterward I asked God to forgive me for this once in a lifetime opportunity that I had missed. At least they knew that Voodoo, emanating out of Bois-Caiman, was no longer king over Haiti. With great admiration; the chief witch doctor followed us all around the city. We continued our informative mission to all the mayor's offices in the region, to the Catholic Archbishop and all the authorities to tell them what God had done through us in Bois-Caiman.

Please, allow me to politely say; shame on some of us Christians! We are afraid of the devil but in reality the devil is afraid of us. Always remember that you are given **"Power to tread on serpents and scorpions, and over all the power of the enemy; and nothing shall by any means hurt you." Luke 10-19**

We are given the Power of Resistance. James exhorts us to: "submit ourselves to God. Resist the devil and he will flee from you." You have no business in doing the fleeing. Make the devil run away in fear. You take control and do the commanding.

NO MORE POWER IN THE VOODOO TREE! WITCH DOCTORS AND GOVERNMENT OFFICIALS PANICKED!

Three days after we returned to Port-au-Prince, the witch doctors and government officials came to the site for their own celebration. They beat their drums and performed all night long under the voodoo tree but lost their power to conjure up the evil spirits. They behaved, as if paralyzed, unable to climb the tree, or to eat glass bottles and make other sacrifices as they had previously done for more than 200 years. They filed a complaint, with the authorities, against us; accusing us with an act of betrayal of the nation's culture.

All the radio and television stations and the newspapers started making a big noise about this. The government called me in many times for interrogation. For more than five weeks, the news media kept calling me for interviews. They wanted to know what we Christians had done to get the government so upset? "For having stymied their praying under the Voodoo Tree in Bois-Caiman," we told them. We used the media to insist on our rights as Haitian born citizens to go anywhere in our country without discrimination. We also claimed equal rights in Haiti.

The same rights the Voodoo people were granted to go to Bois-Caiman for their abominations; so also the Christians should have the same right to go there and pray to their God. The news people asked me, "Why did you go to the Voodoo site? Don't you know that's the devil's territory?" I replied, "The earth is the Lord's and the fullness thereof; the world and they that dwell therein." Psalm 24:1

OFFICIAL VICTORY DECLARATION BY THE GOVERNMENT

So many voices expressed concern with this issue that the government was pressured by its citizens to publish an official media communiqué acknowledging the right of every Haitian to visit any historical site in Haiti. Christians were accorded equal rights to visit Bois-Caiman the same as other groups do. This is an official written victory over the devil in Jesus Name!

A few months later I received official permission, as I had requested, from the government to hold crusades and prayer services at Bois-Caiman. I published that letter in the news to let the whole nation know that there was a historic change in Haiti. The Satanic pact over Haiti had, officially, been broken. Haiti had been liberated!

SATANIC OPPOSITION THROUGH GOVERNMENT OFFICIALS

I would like to warn my brothers and sisters that every victory elicits new opposition. There is no final victory. The Christian life, ministerial life and living itself are constant battlefields. We are called to "fight the good fight of faith" and never to quit. The enemy never quits and never accepts that he has been defeated. The ultimate victory will be when Christ defeats Satan at the battle of Armageddon.

> **When all the kingdoms of the World are become the Kingdoms of our Lord, and of His Christ; and He shall reign for ever and ever. (Revelations 11:15)**
>
> **7 And when the thousand years are expired,**

> **Satan shall be loosed out of his prison,**
>
> **8 And shall go out to deceive the nations which are in the four quarters of the earth,**
>
> **Gog and Ma-gog, to gather them together to battle: the number of whom is as the sand of the sea.**
>
> **9 And they went up on the breadth of the earth, and compassed the camp of the saints about, and the beloved city: and fire came down from God out of heaven, and devoured them.**
>
> **10 And the devil that deceived them was cast into the lake of fire and brimstone; where the beast and the false prophet are, and shall be tormented day and night for ever end ever. Revelations 20:7-10**

After taking the territory for Jesus it was necessary to go back to the area to build up the faith of the new believers in Christ and God's work in Bois-Caiman by returning periodically to preach, teach and organize new crusades.

A few months after that original victory, I requested and obtained an official permit from the central government office in Port-au-Prince and escorted a large contingent from Port-au-Prince and other regions of the country to Bois-Caiman. Among them were a well known, spiritually powerful group named Soldats de Christ led by Frere Jean Claude Oscar. Our meetings were scheduled to last from Sunday to Sunday. I brought with me the official letter of authorization issued by government officials permitting us to hold these meetings at Bois-Caiman.

When we arrived, the city Mayor, the President's regional Delegate and the local police chief rejected the letter; opposing our presence and not allowing us to hold the meetings or minister to the local citizens.

We insisted on our rights as Haitian citizens to be in any territory of Haiti and furthermore we carried authorization papers from the national government to be there. Squads of police were summoned to intimidate us into leaving. We refused to go and continued installing our sound system under the Voodoo Tree. I called on our people to begin worshipping.

At the sound of the first song multitudes of people flooded into the area. That made the police and authorities rethink their efforts and they left, allowing us to have our service.

Every day the delegate and the mayor returned, with the police, asking to cancel the meetings. The chief magistrate summoned me to his office to plead with me, not to conduct prayer on the former Voodoo site. I refused to accede to his requests. The following day, the President's delegate returned to confront us with a larger contingent of police reinforcements. He gave me five minutes to vacate the location. He pronounced, "As the president's direct delegate, I can put you in jail if you do not leave in five minutes." I replied, "Sir, I represent not only the president, but a greater authority than you do. I represent God!" He answered, "Okay. Promise me that you will not pray under the tree." I replied, "Sir, we will conduct these meetings until Sunday night." He left saying nothing more.

After the delegate left, Brother Philemon, a new convert from Bois-Caiman, approached me and offered his private property on which to install the crusade equipment. Doing this we would not be on the government site. I accepted his offer and installed all our sound equipment on his land which adjoins the historical Voodoo site. That night the crowd swelled to nearly 3,000 people from that rural area.

During the worship service the police chief, accompanied by many armed men arrived on the scene in pickup trucks. They jumped out of the trucks and ran to our stage intent to disrupt the service.

These thugs were joined by the mayor and another police chief who served me with a warrant issued by the city magistrate, ordering me to stop the service immediately or be arrested. His armed men set forth unplugging our microphones, musical instruments and public address loud speakers. I removed my watch and my wallet; giving them to my wife and before they disabled the last microphone, I grabbed it and shouted to the crowd, "The mayor is here to shut down the meeting or take to me to jail. I will not stop the meeting, I would rather go to jail, what do you want to do?" They all replied, "All of us will go to prison, but the meeting will not shut down." The crowd of several thousand kept repeating over and over. "We shall all go to prison."

This expression of solidarity by the celebrant masses energized me with such strength and authority that I told the mayor, "I dare you to touch one more thing here! I command you to stop your game right now."

Hearing my bold expression the chief of police grabbed the mayor in hand and both hurried away from our stage followed by all the police officers. Some of my people followed them to hear what they were saying. The police chief told the mayor, "Why did you bring us here? You told us the Christians and Voodoo people were having a bloody fight over the Voodoo Site and asked us to arrest Pastor Jeune. I saw no one fighting; all the people are dancing and worshipping God together."

The mayor insisted, "You must arrest Pastor Jeune!" to which the chief of police answered, "Listen, my mother is one of the most faithful church members; she loves God and prays many times each day. How would she feel to hear that her son had put a pastor in prison for worshiping Jesus?"

He gave his handcuffs to the mayor and told him, "If you want to arrest the pastor, go and do it yourself; as for me, I am out of here!"

While they argued, we continued worshipping and praising God and suddenly we saw the chief of police and all his men returning to their pickup trucks.

We continued worshipping and preaching the Good News of the Gospel. Many people received Jesus that night, others were healed and delivered. This victorious confrontation happened on Wednesday night and God continued to bless us with great services, with no interference, every day and night for the rest of the week.

THEY TRIED WITCHCRAFT POWER AGAINST US

On Thursday night, while we all slept, eight young men brought 12 heads of recently decapitated people. Some people in the area caught them and called the local authorities to deal with this situation. They arrived and said this was part of the culture. They took the young men and the severed heads away with them. Later we were told that the Minister of Interior and those cultural apologists were the ones who sent the young men with their grisly heads to put a death spell on us. Praise God for His power which is greater than their witchcraft power! None of us experienced any negative effect from this voodoo trickery.

A second time they came and put witchcraft tricks under our podium below the very spot where we stood to preach. By the power of God no one was harmed. The testimony we heard was that the witchcraft performers expected some Christians to get hurt. But when they saw none of us got hurt they sent some unsaved people to come by the platform so they could get hurt and that would give them a reason to accuse the Christians. That way we would be accused of causing people's death in the area. They were so surprised that even the unsaved were protected on our ground. The power of the Gospel is so strong and unbeatable.

THE ENEMY NEVER QUITS

Remember that I told you, the enemy never quits. There are no final victories! The Psalmist reminds us that when we go through the Valley of Baca, the Lord leads us from strength to strength. Not if we go, but when we go through it. We know we must go from opposition to opposition, from battle to battle, but also from victory to victory. Before the battle has started, we already know the result. We know on which side the victory is going to be: on God's side, on our side!

> **Blessed is the man whose strength is in thee; in whose heart are the ways of them. Who passing through the valley of Baca make it a well; the rain also filleth the pools. They go from strength to strength, everyone of them in Zion appeareth before God. Ps.84:5-7**

ANOTHER ATTEMPT TO ARREST BISHOP JEUNE RUMORS OF DISAPPEARANCE

While in Bois-Caïman, during the crusade I was invited on Sunday morning, to preach at the OMS Church-4VEH Radio in Vaudreuil. Since the whole service was broadcast live, the government officials heard me preaching in that church over the radio. They dispatched two trucks full of police and armed men, posting them in front at the church waiting for me. When church was over, as the celebrants were leaving the police were asking them; when was I coming out. Some people returned and informed the pastors.

I wanted to go out at any cost, but the pastors and leaders of the church insisted that I should not let them arrest me in front of the church. So they escorted me on a two hour walk down a back road to Bois-Caiman, where we were having the crusade. My people were so glad to have me back safe and free.

The police waited in front of that church all day till at 9:00 p.m. they decided to go to Bois-Caiman and see if I was there. We were just finishing the service when they arrived. They saw me praying for the sick and the new converts. People were dancing before the Lord. They questioned the congregation about how I got out of the church where they were watching for me all day? They reported to the police chief and spread a rumor that Pastor Jeune possesses the power to disappear!

After the service ended that evening; we decided to pack up and return to Port-au-Prince. We learned that, the following morning, armed men were detaining and searching every vehicle and bus leaving Cap-Haitian in the direction of Port-au-Prince. Praise God that we obeyed His voice and left the night before.

Despite all the confrontations, we experienced a wonderful week of ministry. The Lord guided us through a recurring series of conflicts; one battle to another, all won, non violently, by us. The example of these victories empowered, day after day, the faith of the new converts.

By going to Bois-Caiman and standing steadfast in our mission we were, albeit non violently, directly challenging the authority of the president and government.

FIRST ANNIVERSARY OF THE SPIRITUAL CONQUEST OF BOIS-CAIMAN GREATER OPPOSITIONS! IMPRISONMENT AND VICTORY

August 13th and 14th of 1998 being the First Anniversary of the spiritual conquest, for Jesus, of the demonic spirits at Bois-Caiman; we planned on holding another great crusade to celebrate and thank Jesus for the spiritual independence of Haiti.

Three months before the celebratory crusade, we began advertising and mobilizing for it. We mailed announcements to the government and all the churches in Haiti; distributing flyers and posters and publishing the good news on radio, television and in newspapers.

When the national government learned of our intentions, they panicked and expressed their opposition in the public media. Henceforth, we intensified our media advertising to counter their attacks. The local Voodoo officials in Bois-Caiman heard our advertising.

All the Petite Bourgeois officials in the Bois Caiman jurisdiction as well as the President's delegates totally opposed us revisiting their locale. They publicly announced their plan to burn, destroy and kill if any Christian returned to the locality to hold a crusade. Our response: Do what you will we shall, for eight days, hold and complete our crusade at Bois-Caiman from Sunday to Sunday, August 2nd to the 9th.

Having met several times with local pastors of Cap-Haitian, I was assured of their active participation in the crusade. The local citizenry offered me land adjacent to the site, thus we acquired a few acres next to that infamous parcel of land. A few days before the crusades commencement, I held the legal deed, in the name of our church, to our privately owned property.

On the first Saturday of August, while our team, with the assistance of some locals, were cleaning and preparing our property for the crusade, Mr. Bel, the President's Delegate (Regional Governor) and the Mayor Jean Pouce arrived with two trucks full of thugs who proceeded to attack our hardworking and peacefully assembled laborers.

Using gasoline, machetes, clubs and rocks; they destroyed everything on the property. They burned down our little church along with its precious contents of Holy Bibles and song books. In a rampage they tore down our toilet facilities and then, mindlessly out of control, burned down a Seventh Day Adventist church innocently located nearby.

Not satisfied with their vandalism the thugs turned their rage upon anyone working in the vicinity. This violent terrorism was a strategy to spread fear and dissuade everyone from attending the crusade.

Setting fire over our crusade equipment and our little church building

On Sunday, August second at about 8:30 PM, I arrived from Port-au-Prince. I was appalled by all the damage and physical wounds that had been inflicted. Despite the violence and mayhem that had ensued and was threatening the meeting the local pastors and their constituencies held service that opening night but dismissed early.

They informed me that the mayor with some policemen had been waiting to arrest me but impatiently left five minutes before I arrived. Praise God I had been delayed along the way.

In brief I announced the opening of our meeting to take place the next evening on Monday, August the third.

ARRESTED FOR JESUS! IMPRISONED FOR PRAYING UNDER A TREE! JUDGED FOR CASTING OUT DEMON SPIRITS

Early the following evening our crusade team began to set up the sound system, gas powered electrical generators and other equipment for that evenings crusade. Pastors Gregory Joseph, Berthony Paul, Robert Simeon and I proceeded to Cap-Haitian, Lacul du Nord and La Plaine du Nord to report the vandalism and terrorist activities at Bois Caiman to the local judiciary authorities.

All the judges in the area were hiding, not wanting to see us and not wishing to process our legal complaint. We proceeded to Cap-Haitien, the main city located 10 kilometers from Bois-Caïman County.

While in downtown Cap-Haitian, in front of the court house, on our way to speak with the magistrate; the Chief of Police arrived in his pickup truck stopping behind us. He instructed Pastors Berthony, Gregory and I to follow him, on foot, to the nearby police station. We wanted to know what was going on. The answer was all three of us were being arrested at 3:30 PM.

In Prison for Jesus: Bishop Joel Jeune, Pastor Berthony Paul and Pastor Gregory Joseph.

Around 4:00 PM, the same day, while we were locked in jail, another gang of armed thugs brought by the Mayor invaded the crusade site and set fire to everything; burning down both of our generators as well as much of our sound equipment.

Many were beaten up and the police, after brutalizing them, rounded up some of our leaders and crusade workers into their truck and driving away they crossed paths with a big truck and some buses full of people coming from Port-au-Prince to the crusade. They opened fire at the pilgrims causing fear, panic, screaming and chaos. Praise God that no one was killed or wounded.

Shortly after the shooting spree, as they sped away from the scene of their atrocity, two of their vehicle's tires simultaneously exploded. Unable to continue, the police set their prisoners free. We listened to all that was going on in Bois-Caiman over the radio while behind bars in jail.

Prior to but anticipating what might happen to us at the police station; I asked Robert Simeon who would not be arrested, "Robby, can you promise me something?" He was quick to reply, "My Pastor, ask me anything and I will do it." I continued, "Will you promise me that the crusade will continue if and while I'm in prison, no matter what happens?" He assured me, "Pastor, you have my word, go to jail, if you must, in peace. The crusade will go on; nothing will stop it!"

I was so proud of that young man and had such joy in going to jail for the first time in my life, for the testimony of Jesus Christ. Robert Simeon is a young man raised in my church, graduated in Christ For the Nations Institute. He was one of our youth pastors at that time and he volunteer to serve as my personal security guard at the crusade.

Robby returned to the crusade site and shared my request with Pastors Eddy Volcy and Jodel Gedeus, as well as all our other leaders, exciting them to their purpose. Together they prayed and then checked to see which equipment could be salvaged from the fire. The generators as well as some of the other equipment were operable and put into use for the service during the ensuing powerful night for Jesus.

While the crusade and the day time activities were going on in Bois-Caiman, 500 or more people sat in and camped out for three days and nights outside the jail until we were released. They sang, danced, shouted and prayed. Church choirs, musical ensembles, soloists, duos and quartets took turns serenading us from inside the prison courtyard.

All of this action supported us and helped to lift our spirits from Monday through Thursday when we were released. The Christian policemen and women who serve in that station publicly expressed their disagreement of our being imprisoned for praying and preaching under a tree.

After 2 days in the jail transitional quarter (called garde-à-vue or temporary detention room), we were brought to a section of the prison where they keep the violent prisoners.

When these prisoners learned why we were put in prison, they started a riot on our behalf shouting, "No justice here, to put Pastors, men of God in our section where we criminals and violent men are kept". It became so tense that the prison chief was forced to transfer us to a semi-private cell for us alone, until we were taken to court and finally released.

The formal charges brought against us in the Court were:

1) The Crime of betraying our Haitian Culture and our ancestors beliefs.
2) Trespassing on Voodoo Territory.
3) Stealing our ancestors spirits and refusing to bring them back.

Our counter arguments were: We did not commit a crime of betrayal against our ancestors but brought the Creator God to Bois-Caiman to whom our great ancestor Boukman prayed on behalf of his peoples' freedom back in 1791.

We were not trespassing on any Voodoo Territory since all Heritage Locations in Haiti are a Historic Legacy to all Haitians in perpetuity without discrimination. Finally since the whole earth belongs to our creator, Father God; we, as do any other

Haitians, have the right to inhabit that or any other location in our commonwealth.

We have not broken any earthly law by casting out the demon spirits in Bois-Caiman. Boukman, himself fighting for freedom from slavery for his people, recognized the spiritual bondage that the false gods had inflicted and commanded the slaves cast out and forsake those bogus deities. Jesus only taught us how to cast out evil spirits, but not how to bring them back.

The Government officials were overheard to have said, "If we beat on them, they will say they are suffering like Peter and Paul in the Bible. If we try to kill them, they will be glad to say they want to die like Jesus, and they will be recognized by the nation as heroes and martyrs. Let's release them."

The local judge declared that we had committed no violation and was prepared to let us go; however, we refused to be released unless complete freedom was granted to conduct our crusades in Bois-Caiman and all over Haiti.

Finally, totally exasperated, our jailers released us to return to Bois-Caiman and continue our crusade. Night after night the crowd attendance grew bigger until many thousands were coming from far and wide and God performed numerous miracles every evening.

Bishop Joel, like Apostle Paul,jailed for Jesus

God used our prison experience and the awareness by the general public thereof to draw countless numbers together into a greater unity in his family. Pastors and churches of all denominations joined together to pray and speak out demanding our liberation from prison and religious freedom for Haiti.

Vision Haiti leaders arrived from Miami to express solidarity with us. All the Christian organizations and associations spoke up on our behalf. Some lawyer's associations joined in support of our civil rights. Haitian Communities in the United States, Canada and many other countries of the world exerted pressure on the Haitian government to release us immediately, threatening to stop all monetary transfers to Haiti. Other civil rights groups were planning to sit in and block every street and roadway in non violent civil disobedient protest to force the government to release us.

People from all over the world who got the news on Trinity Broadcasting Network (TBN) and other media were praying for us and voiced their concern and solidarity. Many friends and partners from America traveled to Haiti, came to Bois-Caiman to support us, pray and intercede for our release. The leaders of the Haitian Protestant Federation as well as many pastoral associations, Christian and professional organizations and several Senators and Congressmen publicly expressed their solidarity with us and their disapproval of the Government position in persecuting the Christians.

The Bois Caiman Crusade began with just a few people but grew to many thousands by the time it ended on Sunday. God used the persecutions we all had endured to multiply souls into His kingdom.

FINAL CRUSADE NIGHT: MORE PERSECUTION, GREATER VICTORY!

Sunday evening, the final night of the crusade the crowd in attendance reached its peak. It was standing room only by evening during a meeting which began in the early afternoon. Earlier, I was away in Vaudreuil to talk with a well driller about installing a water well on our property for the people of Bois-Caiman.

Arriving late to the meeting, I was very moved to see such a great multitude but was disappointed at how quiet it was. Everybody was hushed and standing still as if paralyzed. Pastor Eddy rushed up to meet me as I arrived. I asked him, "What's going on? Why did you stop the service?" He pointed towards the Voodoo Tree and said, "Look over there, see all those armed men? The Minister of Interior Dr. J.M. is here with many governmental officials, as well as the national television crew. He shut down the service and asked everyone to leave. I was waiting for you to tell me what to do. He not only asked us to shut down everything, but he's watching every move we make."

I didn't speak, a word, to Pastor Eddy but proceeded to the stage and knelt down and prayed; "Oh God, is the Minister of Interior bigger than You are? Does he have greater authority then You? How can he shut down Your meeting by force and You haven't done a thing? What do You want us to do now, Lord? Answer me, for I will not bow down and I will not give up!" I waited on my knees.

After a few minutes, a thought came to me, like a soft voice, that told me, "Stay on your knees and call your crusade team leader. Tell him to have his team ready for quick action. Have the generator, the sound system and a microphone turned on in seconds, all together at the same time." They did exactly what I said.

I quickly got up, took the microphone, jumped up to the pulpit and shouted, "Alleluia! Let everyone here clap their hands to welcome the great chief, Jesus and shout Alleluia!" The multitude of people shouted so loud and often the Minister of Interior covered his ears. I continued, "I just arrived at this meeting after being out searching for someone to drill a well for the people here in Bois-Caiman and have been informed that the Minister of Interior is here; would you like to see him?" The crowd shouted, "Yes, Yes, Yes." Responding to them, I requested the minister to come up to the stage and address the people on behalf of the president. The crowd shouted again, "Yea, Yea, Yea," and started singing and dancing all around the grounds. I called again, louder, "Please, make room for the Minister of Interior to come up to the platform to let the population know the reason that brought him here to be with us."

The minister and his men reacted by running to their vehicles. I urged the pastors in the crowd to go and bring the minister up to the stage.

They went and knocked on the window of his vehicle requesting, "Come with us, the Bishop wants you to talk to the people!" He nervously replied, "Please, let me leave!" His guards proceeded to clear a way out for his vehicle because the narrow road into Bois-Caiman was blocked by vehicles, buses and trucks bringing hundreds more people to the crusade. His men had to cut through some bushes to open a way out and around both the traffic jam and the thousands whose attention had shifted towards him; so he could flee our gathering peacefully.

What a mighty God we Serve! Always with us from one opposition to another; from victory to victory! This was one of the greatest crusades we had ever held. Countless souls were saved and many people were healed and set free.

BATTLE AGAINST VOODOO

After the Minister of the Interior fled the scene, we continued our service until a contingent of witch doctors and government officials arrived to practice their Voodoo blood sacrifice next to the tree. Some of them, I was told, had been part of the delegation that came with the Minister of Interior; which is the reason why they attempted to shut down our meeting and ordered the Christians to leave. The Minister was embarrassed to practice his witchcraft in front of all the Christians. Since he was pressured to leave, he sent some of his men back with the witchdoctors.

The Voodooists began beating on their drums, working up frenzy for the sacrifice. Hearing the drums resounding from beneath the Voodoo Tree, only a few hundred feet from our crusade, and seeing the distraction it was causing in our crowd; a righteous anger came over me and I shouted out, "Devil ! How dare you bring your servants here, to try to give you glory while God is being glorified by His people?"

THE MIRACLE OF THE VOODOO TREE!

I asked the people to stretch out their hands towards the tree and I petitioned God to bring His judgment upon it.

In a few minutes, we all saw a heavy rain falling down on the tree causing the witch doctors and officials to pick up their drums and run away from the tree. We were told later that they ran away because a rain of fire was showering the tree and burning them. In a few months, the misbegotten tree dried up and died, down to its roots. The voodoo tree has been cursed, dead and gone. What a mighty God we serve!

Voodoo Tree before God cursed it

The Voodoo tree after it was cursed.
All other trees around it remain completely green.

STAY FOCUSED ON YOUR CALLING

Upon returning home after the successful first anniversary crusade at Bois-Caiman and the victory in prison; I was met by thousands of people who staged a triumphant march in the streets.

The Port-au-Prince population welcomed me like a victorious general returning from a war. Many asked me to run for president and were ready to campaign and vote for me. I remembered what God had promised my father before I was born and that I was raised from death for His spiritual kingdom, not for an earthly one. I reminded myself that I had to remain humble and focused; just as Jesus had to stay focused when the crowds of people tried to make him a political king.

GOD'S VENGEANCE AND MERCY

In just a few months after these events five of the men who launched the attacks on the Christians, burned the churches and tried to destroy our sound equipment died of rabies. Before these poor deluded men died, they confessed to their crimes and how much they had been paid to participate in these acts of terrorism. The Chief of Police, who had persecuted and incarcerated us, was killed during illegal drug dealings. The Mayor who persecuted us lost his mind, became mentally paralyzed and mysteriously died. The President's Delegate (Regional Governor) got into some serious trouble, was fired and forced to leave the country, his house got burned, he lost his family and everything he got. The Minister of Interior lost his job.

Many of the other men, who had participated in the attacks, got saved when they witnessed God's judgment on their fellow conspirators. They testified about the wrath of God against the power of Voodoo. The witch doctors had sent them armed with plenty of demonically crafted and spell infused objects to deposit around and under our stage during the crusade and could not understand why their spells didn't work and no Christians were harmed. These hired thugs came to realize that God's power is greater than that of the devil and Voodoo; consequently they received Jesus and joined His church.

THE CHURCH OF JESUS VICTORIOUSLY STANDS IN BOIS-CAIMEN

For many years we weren't able to establish a church in Bois-Caiman. Every structure we built had been destroyed by night or day by the mayor's men.

Pastor David Gingrich from Picton, Ontario Canada brought a construction team organized from many Gospel Crusade churches of Canada. This team labored, enthusiastically, to construct a nice church building but the enemy tried to stop them; lying and claiming that the Canadians had torn down the Haitian flag at Bois-Caiman replacing it with the Canadian Maple Leaf banner. When the church was nearing completion, the enemy came one night and destroyed the building leveling it down to the ground.

God gave Pastor David Gingrich a strategy. He and his team prepared a meal and invited the whole community to come and eat. This altruism was meant to establish unity between the Haitians and Canadians.

Conducting a church service upon the foundation of the destroyed building they promised to return as many times as it would take to build a lasting church. On a subsequent trip Pastor David returned with a new team and they constructed another church, unopposed. They increased its size because the congregation waiting to use the building had outgrown the smaller dimensions. The new mayor is now a member of that Bois-Caiman church.

The Church of Jesus Christ in Bois Caiman stands alive, well and strong!

The Beautiful Church of Jesus Christ at Bois Caiman that stands strong as a lighthouse! A gift of Gospel Crusade of Canada

WHAT HAS CHANGED AS A RESULT OF THIS?

Prior to our spiritual campaign, Christians couldn't go to Bois-Caiman; only high officials, Voodoo Witch Doctors and priests were allowed. Now it's different! The atmospheric heaviness people used to feel when they arrived in Haiti is no longer felt. The Voodoo drums our visitors used to hear all night, no matter where they were staying in the country are rarely heard. Fewer people have been attending the Voodoo services or practicing the occult. Less people frequent the cemeteries on the holidays for the dead.

In recent years, prayer meetings have been held in the Presidential Palace every Thursday. There is complete religious freedom throughout Haiti.

More parents purpose to send their children to school to get an education instead of relying on Voodoo and witchcraft to assure their future. People go to church and medical doctors for their healing rather than going to witch doctors. Our national soccer team used to allow witch doctors to bathe their feet before they went to play in a match; now they gather for prayer to God before the contest begins.

When we first arrived at Bois-Caiman in 1997, there were no cement block structures; merely little mud houses. We drilled water wells for the people and now there are nice hotels, expensive homes and beautiful gardens. Young women would have children out of wedlock. Now they marry and get baptized. 90% of the Voodoo population has turned to Jesus! Bois-Caiman currently offers educational facilities from pre-school through high school.

> **For I am not ashamed of the Gospel of Christ: for it is the POWER of GOD unto salvation to everyone that believes." Romans 1:16.**

We have changed our national anthem; now including God in it. When our school children sing the national anthem, they are singing about God, instead of Voodoo. This change has not yet been officially sanctioned by the government but is standard in our Christian churches and schools.

The country's economic status has improved. The literacy rate jumped from 21% to 45%. The life expectancy jumped from 49 to 53 years. The infantile mortality rate was 47% and now is way down. HIV was very high and now is greatly reduced.

In 1978 the State Religion and Voodoo population was 80%;today, according to the most recent religious statistic that was released by the Haiti Research and Statistic Center; the Evangelical Christian population is estimated at more than

51%, the Voodoo population is estimated around 3.11% and the other religions share the balance left.

Another statistic shows 24,000 Evangelical Protestant churches, 4,000 Catholic churches and 400 Voodoo temples in Haiti. One man in the Bible challenged 450 Baal prophets (Witch Doctors); how much more 24,000 of God's power believing Churches can do to 400! We certainly can conquer all for Christ.

During our last crusade in Bois-Caiman, its new mayor and his office staff constituted the praise band, playing musical instruments, donated to the church by Gospel Crusade of Canada, and leading the worship service. The new Chief of Police was the main preacher one night.

So much unity among the pastors was fostered when we all spent time in jail together for Jesus. They weren't interested in attending the spiritual warfare crusades; not wanting to challenge the demons in their territory. As a Christian army, irrespective of denominations, we came together and defeated these demons on the land they were claiming. The excitement created by this victory brought out most of the pastors to our crusades and seminars.

What challenges are you facing at this time of your life? Are you willing to stand in faith with Jesus? Are you willing to resist the devil and watch him flee from you? The result is a product of believing God's Word, persistence and patience: for God Cannot Lie!

WHAT IS GOD DOING NOW THROUGH THE CHURCHES IN HAITI?

As a result of faithful, consistent intercession the churches are experiencing a growth explosion. God's blessing is for all of us and as children of God we have the legal right and sacred duty, in Jesus name, to break the contract our forefathers entered into with Satan; destroying now and for all time the devil's power in Haiti.

God has equipped us with his power to fight and defeat the devil and take back all he has taken from us. We must liberate ourselves from a mentality that the devil has some kind of territory in our lives and lands. This is one of his deceptions. He has no territory! Everything on this earth is God's gift for us! Thank God for the victory He gave us. We want and will get ALL the stolen territories back from the devil.

Most Haitians now reject the power of demons and are accepting Christ as their personal Savior. The last official statistics published about religious groups in Haiti, show that the Voodoo population has declined to 31 percent, down from 80 percent in 1978!

Many Voodooists had trouble birthing children. They experienced spontaneous abortions, eventually coming to believe that the devil was responsible for their misfortunes. They were losing their children, some even after being born, because of the witchcraft they were involved in.

After receiving Christ into their lives; families experienced normal, healthy child births. Voodoo is a destructive curse. Jesus is a creative and constructive power. There are many reasons to reject belief in the devil.

We have opened more Christian schools who teach scriptures to the witch doctor's children. Thus the belief in the devil is fading away as they learn about, turn to and believe in God. Biblical education is making a difference in winning hearts and minds for God.

The political situation is now more problematic than Voodoo because once the Voodooists know we are Christians and understand the power of God, they fear us. They may try to hinder our work but the Lord always delivers us a victory.

The Haitian economy is very bad and the government seems confused and unable to understand what we are doing. They don't want us to accomplish much but paradoxically want us to do more. They are very possessive of their political power; not wanting us to be popular with the people even though we are working for the common good.

Customs and their exorbitant tariffs, in Haiti, have been a great and ongoing challenge. It has been very difficult to get donations from the States released. We have lost many containers. It is a difficult situation but the Lord has helped us and we thank God for sending Missionaries; American, Canadian and others, to assist us physically and financially. These Godly brothers and sisters also help us during Crusades and Pastor's Seminars. In Unity, we are overcoming.

We broke Satan's strongholds through intercessory prayer by going into his captive territories in the name of Jesus. When people give Christ their hearts and Jesus comes into their lives, the power of Satan is broken. Both powers cannot co-exist in the same space. When the light shines in, the darkness must depart; thus overthrowing Satan and elevating Jesus as king.

WITNESS TO WITCH DOCTORS

We send out groups to witness to the witch doctors; usually going to the Voodoo temples. Most of the time the beating on the Voodoo drums will stop and the Voodooists will listen to our witness. Even if the Voodooists do not get saved, they are assured that we will be praying for them and that they will in time come to Jesus. Now we have little resistance from the Voodoo people. They accept being preached and witnessed to.

CHAPTER 10

Leadership
Inspiring Others To Achieve

I always share the visions that God gives me with my leaders. I start from nothing but t0he faith and vision that God blesses me with. This is an example for many of the pastors who go out and enlarge their tents, their churches and their vision. Sometimes they say it is my fault they dream big, because I encourage them to think big through my teaching. God is bigger than your circumstances; let him draw you to a higher place. He is a big God so dream big. I have seen the results of that. I give my blessing to many of the young pastors who ministered with me encouraging them to go out and start another ministry. I believe that God has used me to encourage the younger generation, to assume their holy responsibilities and in doing so to make sure that God blesses them and their country, abundantly.

One of the joys of my life is training up new pastors; all the pastors who minister alongside me have been raised up in our ministry. I believe there is no success without a successor. I want to make sure, because it is the will of God, there will be some good successors who will carry on the work of this ministry. The ministry must go on, even if Doris and I are no longer here.

The Joshua generation in God's hand: Hope for a brighter future

I also thank God for His wisdom and the ability He bestowed upon me to mentor and train the next generation. I believe the church in Haiti has a brighter future with the next generation as they learn to allow the Holy Spirit to guide and empower their lives.

The children's education is the nation's future

Jonathan Joel Jeune with Grand-Pa Joel Jeune

Why should I worry about the future? When the time comes for me to sleep, the new and next generation's eyes will be wide open, ready to accomplish great things for God and even greater things than I could ever have done in my lifetime.

LEADERSHIP MEANS GROWTH

We put emphasis on three levels of growth: spiritual, functional, and numerical. Leadership is one of the keys that helps. We have a method to educate church members to become leaders and then in turn to train others to assume leadership. After attaining leadership status, they help the pastor care for the flock. When the flock is well cared for they are empowered to invite other sheep, to come in.

We are very strong in prayer, intercession, evangelism and witnessing. Through these four areas and lots of teaching the Word of God, we inspire our congregants to their responsibility of winning souls to Christ. I believe these are contributing reasons for my success in raising up strong leaders.

After the church expanded to 3,000 people, I attended a leadership seminar in South Korea (Pastor Paul Yonnge Cho) and learned a method of making my work easier. Upon returning, with this newly acquired knowledge, I focused on training leaders; spending lots of quality time with them. Using these new organizational methods I trained 500 leaders; then I divided the church by alphabetical order. Leaders were placed in sectional groupings (sections A, B, C, etc.) problems or ideas remained in these groups or sections to be addressed first by its leaders.

When big problems arise and a decision cannot be reached they bring the matter to me. We have twelve pastors in our mother church, at Waney and over 350 elders, deacons and other leaders making it possible for me to have mobility; as the Lord leads or the church needs.

At Grace Tabernacle, our church within Grace Village at Lamentin 52, we have 7 pastors and over 150 deacons and other leaders.

We have wonderful, dedicated, Christian brothers and sisters administering and staffing the schools, Bible school, orphanages and widows' home. Our evangelistic outreach is spreading the Gospel throughout the country.

Before God spoke to me, as he did to Moses, I tried to do everything myself. Now I can have several crusades going on and only be in attendance if I have to. Planning and organization helps the work continue in my absence, to my relief.

I pour my heart and soul into leadership; training one group after another in two year programs. Constantly expanding our training; we create courses on various levels to prepare our people for the work of their calling. Level five is the pastoral level.

The Lord has been good to me. While he's made me soft, He has made Doris, my wife, very tough; so that when there is a difficult situation, I often turn my wife loose and she deals with it. My father on the other hand, while also loving people and being compassionate, was very tough.

While growing up, I asked God, "Lord, I would like to be a little softer." I believe God gifted me with greater compassion but not to the detriment of God's work. When it comes time to stand up to the enemy, nothing will stop me from doing so. Like David I'm ready for any Goliath.

I do, somehow, find time to relax. Sometimes I play music, study or watch a video tape, miracle or action movie for relaxation and, of course, when I am very tired; I try to get some sleep.

I am an early riser, so at 5 AM I have to get up. I love to play with the children at the girls' and boys' homes. We all have so much fun together playing with them which is relaxing for all of us. I still play piano and accordion and used to play trumpet but don't have time to practice and maintain my chops (embouchure) on the horn. I have always participated in sports with my sons and play table tennis and volleyball.

Pastor Doris and I have made up our minds to trust God for every need. He has been so faithful from the very beginning; taking us through the wilderness so many times unto miraculous breakthroughs. He has given us the leadership spirit to encourage and help others. I believe God is our source of encouragement and of victory over any attacks of the enemy.

I am encouraged when attending leadership seminars during which pastors share their concerns, needs and burdens thus realizing that we are not alone in the race. We are encouraged by each other and by the visions that God gives us.

The Haitian political instability has slowed our program of evangelism. There are places where one cannot go and others that are very difficult to get access to, due to bad roads and lingering violence. During times of political instability, the churches of Haiti send teams to go door-to-door witnessing. They hold open air meetings, conduct family outreach, stage crusades and show films.

UNITY IS THE KEY

In the past, it has been very difficult to work with some non-Pentecostal churches but we know that unity is the key to victory. When we began praying together, many of them were very reluctant to come. They did not want to mix with any

Spirit-filled people but when we commenced having crusades; their members came to see what was going on.

They came because they liked the way we worshipped. When they brought this spirit of worship with them to their former churches, their pastors attempted to suppress this spiritual energy so many of their congregants left these, lukewarm, churches and migrated to fellowships where worship was vibrantly alive.

In an attempt to retain their members these churches now try to conduct worship like we do and that helps them hold onto their congregants. This fosters a communality of worship among all the churches and strengthens the unity among them.

Strong unity among the pastors was fostered when we all spent time in jail together. Initially they weren't interested in attending the crusades; being reluctant to challenge the demons in their territory. As a Christian army, irrespective of denominations, we came together and defeated these demons on the land they were claiming. The excitement created by this victory encouraged most of the pastors to attend our crusades.

LEADERS CAN LEARN FROM MISTAKES BE SPIRITUALLY WISE AND BE CAREFUL

A pastor in my fellowship had his own way of seeking God's will for every move he made. The way he did it was to close his Bible and his eyes; then, with eyes closed, open the Bible and place a finger on a page. The randomly selected scripture his finger landed on would, by his quasi divination method, be interpreted as God's latest command to him. He used this method for a long time in his ministry.

One day while he was going through a very tough situation in his life, he told God, "Lord I am tempted to commit suicide, if you do not help me out of this trouble immediately". He demanded an instant answer from God and resorting to his finger divination he landed on Matt.27:5 and read ". . . he departed, and went and hanged himself." Fearfully dismayed he repeated his finger prophetic methodology and once again his thoughtless finger led him astray as it added once again a part of a scripture to his mixed up request for an answer; this time John 13:27 ". . . that thou doest, do quickly."

Interpreting these unrelated scriptural fragments to be a confirmation from God for him to commit suicide he went to submit his misguided resignation to our District Superintendent Pastor. He asked to be replaced by another man because God had commanded that he kill himself.

Blessedly, his more spiritually level headed superintendent prayed some Godly wisdom into the errant brother, with the carnal finger, and helped him to change the way he was foolishly trying to find the will of God.

So be careful of leaning on your own understanding and trying to hear God's voice through fragmented bits and pieces of scripture which the voice of another might use to trick you and mock God's word.

I also have made some mistakes in my life, like dealing with some of my leaders. I think, however, that there are lessons that I can teach to some of the younger leaders. We can all learn from our mistakes but there aren't too many things that I would change. I can, from my own experience and God's leading, share with others how to deal with situations correctly and in doing so, overcome adversities when they arise.

As for the stand I took against Voodoo, I have no regrets because it had to be done. When the Lord tells you to do His will in a situation, you must obey, lest he find someone else. Standing up against governments and others to overthrow witchcraft and idolatry has long been God's will and I will always step into the breach for Him and do it again. The Lord has been leading my steps and I thank Him for that.

A WORD OF WISDOM TO FOREIGN MISSIONARIES

I have witnessed and then helped resolve many conflicts between foreign missionaries and Haitian Nationals but some ended up being litigated in the courts. What happens most of the time is unclear vision and lack of communication.

In Haiti we have too many abandoned churches, schools and orphanages because of unresolved conflicts. How do we avoid such divisiveness within the Kingdom of God? Though I cannot offer a formulaic solution for every situation; I can share some of my own experiences.

My ministry suffered from a terrible conflict that occurred, for many sad years, between a large Christian Organization and us. Rather than resolving the dispute with Jesus admonitions to guide them, they took us into Haiti's civil courts. That organization purposed to assist us in the building of a particular project. We had already purchased the land and were making payments on it. When that organization offered to help raise some of the funds to build the project; we had no idea they might have ulterior motives and that they would want to co-opt the project for themselves; to become the owner. Many individuals, churches and organizations contributed funds to that project; freely giving, with no strings attached. The situation was ugly to the unsaved people in Haiti; discouraging many of them from coming to Christ.

How could such a situation been prevented? Here are 12 commandments to avoid conflict:

1) If you have a call to a mission for another country, make your vision clear and be honest and transparent about your intentions.
2) If part of your vision is to own property in building your ministry; reveal your ownership intentions from the beginning.
3) In order to purchase land in Haiti you must register your organization with either the Ministry of Religious Affairs, Department of Education or Department of Social Affairs; depending on the nature of the project you have in mind to implement. You must also have a Haitian, resident citizen, appointed as its Director to submit for registration and then to oversee your project. As soon as you are approved and licensed to do so, you may acquire the property, for your project, in the name of your organization.

4) You must make it clear by an MOU (Memorandum of Understanding) whether you intend to assist another ministry or to own the land outright. If you intend to assist then you're designated a working partner with that country's citizen(s) national(s).
   If, and when, your organization is legally registered and becomes eligible to acquire the property it is seeking for its project then it will be able to own it. Haitian citizens can work, with you, as associate(s).
5) You cannot own any property somebody already purchased, or any ministry or citizen national of that country already acquired, unless they have the legal right to sell it to your organization which, of course, must be duly registered with the Government of Haiti.
   Otherwise, you can only partner with or assist them. You cannot legally reclaim your donation.
6) It cannot be a Master-Servant relationship. Make sure there is brotherly and mutual respect, consideration, honesty and transparency. It is much better to keep a Macedonian Call missionary type. In Acts 16, the Apostle Paul had a vision of a Macedonian calling. "Come over and help us!" This remains as the best model for missionary relationships.
   The Apostles never owned any properties in the mission field. They went out and established churches; trained and ordained leaders to build on their foundational work and then moved on to other mission fields.
7) If your organization enters into a partnership with an existing local organization; all fundraising for its operations should be jointly conducted and all expenses incurred would need to be transparently reported to the ministry associates.
8) Do not make any promise you may not be able to keep.
9) Fix problems as soon as they arise, do not allow them to become mountains, impeding your ministry.
10) Maintain a spirit of forgiveness with each other. Everyone, occasionally, makes mistakes. Prayer and

reconciliation will keep your ministry and relationships from derailing.

11) Do not make unreasonable demands of each other.
12) Learn and respect the culture of the country you are ministering in.

CHAPTER 11

For Haiti's Brighter Tomorrow
Haiti's Glorious Past

The Island of Haiti was one of the most beautiful and prosperous Islands in the western hemisphere. As mentioned earlier in this book, it was called "the Pearl of the Antilles." Haiti is the first nation in the world in which slaves of African origins rebelled and created an independent republic and, after the United States, the second liberated nation in the Americas.

Bishop Jeune in front of the HEROES of INDEPENDENCE Statutes in Cap-Haitian

This newly independent nation helped many other countries in South America like Bolivia, Venezuela and others to gain independence and proclaim their national freedom.

Haiti's assistance for the American's struggle for independence during their revolutionary war with England was significant.

The battlefield pictures shown below commemorate the Haitian contribution to that struggle; with messages etched onto the sides of the monuments in Savannah Georgia.

Dr Joel Jeune standing in front of Haitian Soldier's monument at Savannah, GA.

Haitian Heroes

Inscription Tablets on Haitian Soldiers Monument seen below.

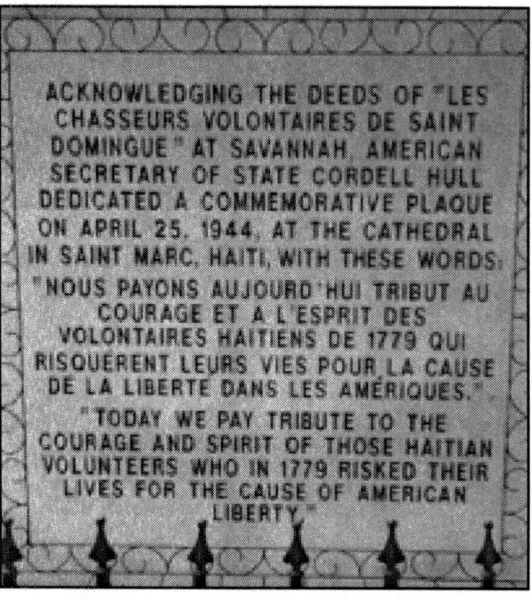

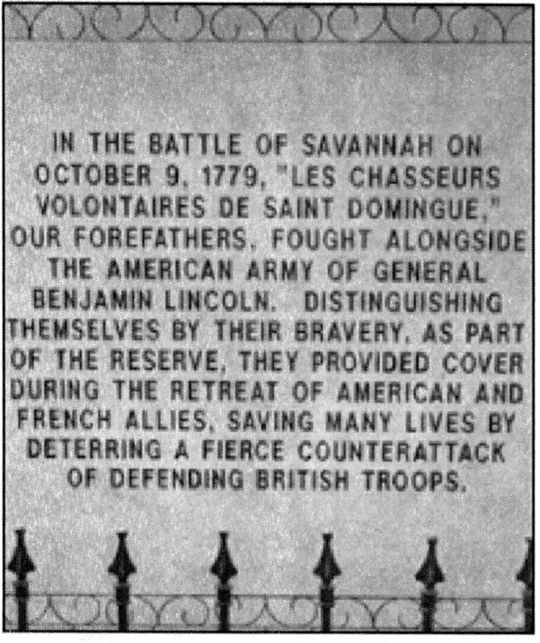

IN ITS FOURTH YEAR, THE AMERICAN REVOLUTION HAD BECOME AN INTERNATIONAL CONFLICT. REBELLING AMERICAN COLONIES AND THEIR FRENCH ALLIES ATTEMPTED TO CAPTURE SAVANNAH FROM THE BRITISH IN 1779. HAITIAN SOLDIERS OF AFRICAN DESCENT WERE PART OF THE ALLIED FORCES. FOLLOWING THE BATTLE, MANY OF THESE HAITIANS WERE DIVERTED TO OTHER MILITARY DUTIES, RETURNING TO THEIR HOMES YEARS LATER, IF AT ALL. SEVERAL VETERANS OF THE CAMPAIGN BECAME LEADERS OF THE MOVEMENT THAT MADE HAITI THE SECOND NATION IN THE WESTERN HEMISPHERE TO THROW OFF THE YOKE OF EUROPEAN COLONIALISM.

ALTHOUGH HUNDREDS OF OTHER "CHASSEURS VOLONTAIRES" REMAIN ANONYMOUS TODAY, A NUMBER OF THEM ARE DOCUMENTED AND LISTED BELOW.

PIERRE ASTREL; LOUIS JACQUES BEAUVAIS; JEAN-BAPTISTE MARS BELLEY;
MARTIAL BESSE; GUILLAUME BLECK; PIERRE CANGÉ;
JEAN-BAPTISTE CHAVANNES; HENRI CHRISTOPHE; PIERRE FAUBERT;
LAURENT FÉROU; JEAN-LOUIS FROUMENTAINE; BARTHÉLEMY-MÉDOR ICARD;
GÉDÉON JOURDAN; JEAN-PIERRE LAMBERT; JEAN-BAPTISTE LÉVEILLÉ;
CHRISTOPHE MORNET; PIERRE OBAS; LUC-VINÇENT OLIVER;
PIERRE PINCHINAT; JEAN PIVERGER; ANDRÉ RIGUAD;
CESAIRE SAVARY; PIERRE TESSIER; JÉROME THOBY; JEAN-LOUIS VILLATE

WE HONOR ALL OF THEIR COLLECTIVE SACRIFICES, KNOWN AND UNKNOWN.

Savannah Battle Monument

The mutual friendship and collaboration between the nations of Haiti and America has been strong since the beginning of our History. We are thankful for the solidarity and the ties that bind our neighboring countries together.

POLITICS AND THE HAITIAN CHURCH

The early Christian message in Haiti was that politics is akin to a capital sin. Talking about politics was thought to be a direct ticket to hell; that Christians should not vote, since Jesus is our President, Law Maker, King, Master and Leader. All churches taught that in the event someone criticized the president and was killed as a result of it, the mistake was theirs for they should not have been outspoken in their opinions.

At an early age, the Lord instilled a resistance to the status quo within me. In my spirit, I felt a conviction to challenge that repression of free speech.

I was raised in the mountains in the Thiotte Region, near the Dominican Republic border. Even though we were not involved in politics, my dad was somewhat of a community activist. He would take his children and his church members, to fix roads and do other helpful work. He said if a truck turned over because of the bad roads, we, as Christians, were responsible to go and help fix the situation. Often times he would visit the jailed prisoners bringing them food and spiritual sustenance. We were a very community active family.

Consequently, with this family background in my life, I became increasingly concerned about the disaster that was informing and negatively affecting the quality of life as well as the spirit and soul of the people of Haiti. Conducting blood sacrifices during witchcraft rituals at the National Palace our governmental leaders were dedicating the country to Voodoo through their demonic activities. In sanctioning random killings and assassinations of their opponents they were creating a culture of fear. This pervasive corruption of the national morale is contrary to God's will for our citizens and country.

Being cognizant of the nature of liberation struggles in other countries especially the United States, with its foundation of faith; I became aware that all successful outcomes were a result of including God in the body politic. The biblical Daniel tells us that God chooses the kings (leaders) and puts them in authority over their lands. God's word reminds us that when Kings and their people turned to God their lands were blessed but if they turned away from Him they invited curses upon themselves.

By praying and believing God for Godly Christian leaders, I and others of like minded persuasion became involved in the process of spiritual collaboration with Him to foster positive change in Haiti.

We are claiming leaders who will institute just laws, for all, based on Godly principles and reflecting the aspirations of the citizenry to live peacefully with equal opportunities and pursue personal happiness in a healthy environment. Now the leaders of our nation are beginning to work with God.

The government makes the laws that affect everything that I do. If that elected body operates in the realm of darkness while I operate in the kingdom of light I must not stand by and allow my government to continue to function in this misguided way. I must never concede the darkness an opportunity to have power over my life. I believe, as a Christian, that the more of God's light that shines forth upon us, with the word of the Lord informing our lives, the community we reside in will be better. That is why we must get more involved in trying to elect Christian leaders in our country.

We must hold our leaders accountable for their actions. As Christians we must let His light shine through us and spread His word to our fellow citizens thus creating a better community.

We anticipate victory in the natural because it is ours already in the spirit realm. Many locations in Haiti are devoid of the Voodoo power that Witch Doctors and Voodooist officials once nurtured there. Once the demonic spirits are fully overcome, God will bless Haiti and install Christian leaders.

We believe that God is using Christians to change Haiti and turn the country over to Him. When that happens He will pour out His blessings and love; casting out all the poverty and misery; bringing unity to the nation. Haiti shall be born again as a new "Pearl of the Antilles"; better than before.

Bishop Jeune holding hands with the Mayor of Carrefour dedicating the country to God

I respect God and know that if we follow Him and believe His prophecy and what it reveals to us we can help move the country toward His intent for it.

Within this process of transformation, God wishes to do miracles in the area of infrastructure. He desires to change the mentality of His people; not to believe in or follow Voodoo or other abominations but to realize that His is the only answer.

When a country is founded on Godly principles it must succeed, because His word tells us, "Blessed is the nation whose God is the Lord."

Bishop Jeune meeting with the Haiti's Prime Minister And the Minister of Foreign Affairs

Bishop Jeune and Dr. Luke Weaver praying With the Prime Minister

With God's wisdom and power we can influence the public life of our country. We must accept our responsibility to be His light bearers and the salt of the earth that Jesus intends us to be. It's not easy but this is a significant part of our assignment and the churches' mandate.

God's people must rise up to go into and pray over all the remaining high places, casting out the demons, just as we did at Bois-Caiman, thus nullifying all the blood sacrifices that have corrupted the National seat of Power.

During the past few years Christians have been allowed to hold prayer meetings in the National, Presidential Palace every Thursday afternoon. This is a good start to the process of change but we need to be engaged in a more important battle. I feel that I will be one of the men who will go and plead the blood of Jesus over the Haitian Palace; transforming it into a Holy Space within which prayer can Spiritually empower that change.

That Palace shall, with God's anointing grace, become a seat of His righteous power and prayer.

Bishop Jeune greeted with much respect by high Government officials

Bishop Jeune giving the key of the city to Government Officials

I also had the privilege of meeting with several Presidents, Senators and House representatives of Haiti and heads of States in other countries including the United States.

One of my greatest goals is for every last vestige of Voodoo to be eradicated from the Peoples Haitian National Palace and that it shall become a spiritual lighthouse for our country. I believe that God will bless me to see this come to pass and to see our president worshipping God, instead of Voodoo. We want Voodoo exposed, on national television, for what it really is and witness repentance which will turn all of Haiti to God!

MY MESSAGE FOR HAITI'S FUTURE

I tell everyone, in Haiti, who will listen, about the power of God. Sharing my testimony about how God raised me up from death; how a country that was a bastion of Voodoo has changed and is swiftly coming to God. Satan's power is diminishing and God's kingdom is being established in every nation so that the devil will not be tolerated anywhere on God's earth.

Training Leaders is an ongoing ministry

Many Haitians, now ashamed of having once been Voodooists, are leaving the demonology behind to accept Christ. Previously they talked about and identified with Voodoo; now they are saying, "Only God can save Haiti!"

Many children are growing up with the Gospel. We believe that we will have Christian leaders who will dedicate this country to God. This change has already begun. We claim Haiti for the Lord because we believe the day is approaching when Haiti will, by its political leaders, officially be declared a Christian nation.

REVIVAL IN HAITI

Years ago one would hear the sound of Voodoo drums virtually everywhere. Now, one is far more likely to hear Christian songs and the sounds of Christian's worshipping and praying; especially noticeable coming from all directions when standing on the roof of ones house. There are some villages and areas from which Voodoo has disappeared. The Gospel is spreading and increasing numbers, quite possibly a majority, of people are serving God.

In a country like Haiti which was sold to the devil, who brings only curses and denies wealth and blessings, it is necessary to attend to spiritual concerns. After Haiti turns to God, there will follow an economic revolution. The United States was founded on Godly principles and consequently blessed by Him. Haiti was founded on demonic principles and could not, for 200 years, be blessed.

We have seen some good examples of change. There was a village that rejected having any church in its community but when we finally installed one in its midst; the humble little huts, in merely two years, were upgraded to solid, hurricane resistant cement block homes. Now, that little village is transformed and developed with little evidence of its former decrepit condition.

The Gospel informs, instructs and enlightens, telling us, **"Seek ye first the kingdom of God and His righteousness; and all these things shall be added unto you . . ." (Matt: 6:33)**

Surely if we make this our priority the political situation will change and the economic situation will improve. We cannot call ourselves a "Christian Nation," until we put Christ first in our personal and collective lives.

MY THINKING HAS CHANGED

The Lord has been dealing with me because in Haiti, we had always believed that even the word politics was a "capital sin" and that Christians should not vote. A Christian could not become a mayor, a senator or hold any other elective office. Into this mindset I was raised by my father and that's how the body of Christ in Haiti originally thought.

The Word of God relates to us that kings (read in the Book of Daniel), were chosen by God or overthrown by Him. Good and righteous kings brought God's blessings to their domains but when the kings were bad, they attracted curses upon their countries. By these qualities the kings had complicity with the blessings or curses that lifted up or brought down their countries.

Even after considering the history and Godly foundation of the United States and how the Lord was changing other countries through their Christian movements, leaders and presidents; we still wanted nothing to do with politics.

Most pastors in Haiti were taught by their mentors and elders that Christians should not involve themselves in any form of politics. I wouldn't even discuss or discourse about politics.

In 2005 a missionary from Canada confronted me in my church with a provocative notion. His idea was that God's people should rise up and change their political environment; get involved and focus Gods light unto the darkness. I was totally against this thinking and said, "Why is he speaking such absurdities in my church? We don't believe in that."

I was about to take the microphone and refute him when a voice spoke in my mind saying, "When you get up, sing the song that will inaugurate the Christian government." These words resounded so powerfully inside me. I was sure it was Satan besetting my brain and countered the perceived attack, "Satan, I rebuke you in the name of Jesus! We don't believe in earthly governments."

Suddenly, I was struck by the worst stomach ache I had ever experienced rendering me unable to speak. All I could do was cry and the voice continued, even louder, telling me to "sing the inaugural song of the new Haiti's Christian government." I continued to hear this voice ordering me over and over and my stomachache grew worse, so, thinking this might really be God speaking, I pleaded, "Okay Lord, if you're trying to tell me something, please let me know what it is."

Suddenly, the entire congregation rose up in the Spirit. They started prophesying, "Our God has changed our situation and the condition of Haiti. Haitians are now God's people. God does not want any more Voodooists, possessing those red handkerchiefs (symbols of Witch Doctors) in their pockets, to rule over His people.

The ministers and officials routinely use a Voodoo infected red handkerchief to wipe off their chairs before they sit down. "No more red handkerchief leaders. God wants Godly leaders for His people."

I was still crying and hurting all over. The church felt as if on fire. I cried out, "Lord, I receive this message."

I forced myself up to the podium, took the mike and started singing the song, "Grand Dieu, nous te benisons!" Oh God, we bless thy name; we celebrate thy glory; we give our life and our land to Thee." As soon as I opened my mouth to sing this with the congregation, my stomach ache left me. This was a sign for me that God really wanted to change the spiritual situation of our country. Two months later, I shared my experience with some pastors and their congregations. My candidness opened me up to learning about the Christian Movement for a New Haiti which was already doing some civic activities in the churches. No one had previously informed me of this movement because it was well known how I felt about such activities and how I spoke out against politics and political activism on the radio. One of the Movements leaders approached and told me what God had been doing; how 17 pastors were praying for me to be involved and how other pastors were praying and encouraging

Christians to also be involved and consider voting for Godly leaders. Some of those pastors were friends of mine but never told about what was going on because they were afraid of how I might react.

It is amazing how quickly Christians changed their attitudes about politics and voting. In our last election Christians turned out and voted in an overwhelming way. It is amazing how God is reversing their old ideas and prompting them into taking a stand and voting Christian leaders into office.

We must shine His light unto the world. We cannot let the darkness rule over us and expect the country to become what we want it to be. God's guiding light should inform the leaders of our country because they draft our laws and decide so much that will impact all of us in Haiti.

It is amazing how God is teaching our Haitian people new ways of relating to their society. The new 'Body Politic' is beginning to elect Christian leaders. The people are lifting up God in Spirit based pragmatic ways. We believe God creates leaders and removes the petit anti Christ's among us.

GOOD ELECTIONS ARE OUR FUTURE

Praise God! Recent elections, beginning in 2006, produced encouraging results as a majority of voters chose many Christian senators, congressmen, mayors, and others to represent them in local and national government. We are witnessing the onset of great changes in Haiti. The country is now safer for visitors and missionaries to visit. Violence and kidnappings have declined. To God be the glory!

I believe that more political leaders will turn to God. The message to all in Haiti is that God remains, as he was yesterday, is today and will always be, the only answer. The devil's day is done, his power over Haiti is broken. The season of good elections has arrived and we shall, in time, elect a Christian majority just as the people of Uganda have done. This is God's time for the nations.

Those who have ambitions for public office must be shown that Voodoo power is null and void and can contribute nothing to ensure them victory. They must learn that if they want to succeed and be recognized, they must accomplish their goals, honestly and truthfully, through democratic elections. That if they lie to the people the electorate will not vote for them. If they earn the trust of the people, they will win elections. I don't believe that people who trust in Voodoo will have a chance anymore but it is very difficult right now with extensive political fighting. Sooner or later, we Christians shall be victorious because we are steadfast in our Faith and audacious in our hopes.

My life, as well as many pastors' lives, has been threatened. Many journalists and politicians were forced to flee the country. It is very dangerous because the opposition usually dispenses with any legal charges against Christians; just sending out gangs of assassins and terrorists to kill and spread fear. Some pastors homes have been burned down; except in Bois-Caiman our buildings have remained protected and we believe God will continue to shelter us from harm's way.

THE FAVOR OF GOD

We have experienced the favor of God and believe it will be with us in all of our endeavors. Our heartfelt desire is to be a blessing to the people of Haiti so that our motherland will shine, as an example, to the rest of the world; especially countries which have experienced similar trials and tribulations as ours; of what God, through His people, can accomplish.

God's message of hope has been extensively announced to the people of Haiti and they believe it. Increasingly they are saying that only God can save and deliver Haiti. The rich and socially upper class citizens who have no material disadvantages are also looking to God. Convicted, of their Spiritual lack, they are turning to prayer. Sometimes, they learn about what God is doing in other countries and become encouraged to put their hope in God; coming to believe in the power of prayer.

From customs to the bureau of motor vehicles and most other major or minor governmental departments corruption is entrenched. One needs God's wisdom to deal effectively with these petite bureaucrats; being careful of what to say or not to say and when and where to be or not to be. It is government as theatre of the absurd; an "Alice in Wonderland" officialdom requiring careful navigation through a gauntlet of mad hatters picking your pocket for all they can extort. A very delicate situation, not easily dealt with while maintaining ones Christian composure. One must pray and stay cool.

Our ministry is in Haiti, so I must rely totally on God's protection. The United States Department of State has a permanently issued warning for American citizens not to travel to Haiti because it is not safe to do so. Missionaries, North American and European relatives of Haitian Nationals and concerned friends of Haiti, all undaunted by the well founded warnings of kidnappings, persist on traveling to our country; bringing gifts of goodwill and volunteer labor. Prayer, precautions, wisdom and good common sense should always be exercised in Haiti.

There are times not to venture into the streets and areas that are never safe to set foot in so that even the police don't try. There have been kidnappings of American and French citizens, even Haitian children. You just have to believe God will protect you.

A BRIGHT FUTURE BY FAITH

By our abiding Faith, Haiti's future outlook is bright with God's promise. He shall deliver us from the chaos spawned by our past mistakes and our country's present transitory confusion. God will raise up new leaders who, with the support of a spiritually enlightened body politic, will steer Haiti's future course with His principles. With God's blessings our people will reap the finances to meet their families' needs. Hunger, decrepit living conditions and untreated illness will no longer lead them to angrily burn tires in the streets or commit violence upon their fellow citizens. With God's help Haiti will change. This is the hope of all Christians. This is our prayer.

We have faith in God and know He sustains us in Haiti because our motherland will change and because we are His servants, His instruments for a new beginning, because we are His children. Possessing our own limited and humble abilities we must lean on and depend upon Him. Christians are praying and hearing God saying, "No more! Enough is enough!. Enough Voodoo! Enough corruption!" We keep the faith, hope and assurance that change will come soon. WE SHALL OVERCOME!

Through our several yearly crusades, thousands receive the positive and life transforming message.

MY FUTURE

My future is in God's hands and with His guiding light I see myself continuing to serve His people. I see my battle with the Haitian Palace and its hierarchy, not as leader or president but one whom God will give access to reform; to go into and pray over, as we did in Bois-Caiman, and cast the demons out. We can nullify all the blood sacrifices that have corrupted the national seat of power. During the past few years Christians have been enabled to hold prayer meetings in the Palace every Thursday afternoon. A good start but we need to be engaged in a bigger battle. I feel that I will be one of the men, who helps spiritually empower that change in Haiti.

We have a plan to reach everybody in Haiti. God is telling me there is a transition of power coming. He is installing His people to higher positions just as he did in days of yore, in Daniel and Joseph's time. We used to believe for less but now the church must be prepared for a new day dawning. God is going to turn over many governments of the world to His people.

The scripture says, 'We shall not be the tail, we shall be the head.' This is coming to pass in many countries.

It is a time of transition and God's people are ready for change. His Gospel is for all of humanity, not just the poor but for all who are poor in spirit. What He asks of us is to include His Word in every aspect and area of our personal lives as well as the collective life of our communities and by extension our country as a whole. In any and every stage of life the people of His Creation cross paths with opportunities to know about and receive Jesus. No one really has an excuse. When all have heard about Him, Jesus will return.

THE SUFFERING MUST END!

The Devil has inflicted massive suffering upon my people. Satan's agenda, to steal, kill and destroy; against my fellow Haitians is why I am so committed against that Devil.

Jesus has been so good to me. He resurrected me from the dead and gave me life more abundant; doing so much for my family and me. I love Him so much. My heart's desire is for His kingdom to reign supreme and for His Name to be above all others. May He be glorified in every home and by every tongue. May every knee bend before Him. My burden for my nation is that all my brothers and sisters will be free; spiritually, economically and socially. I want my country of Haiti to have good infrastructure and that our citizens live like those of civilized countries and that they attribute their blessings to God and glorify Him.

CHAPTER 12

Haiti's Children
My Heart's Cry

Many years ago my wife and I started orphanages to care for children in need. Our hearts have been with the children since we began our ministry 40 years ago.

My wife Doris was raised in Sunshine Home orphanage since she was 5 days old. At the age of 14, she was brought to the Gospel Crusade orphanage which was built and run by Pastor Henry Brunk and Dr Gerald Destine. I met her at that orphanage where she lived until we married.

As we prepared to get married, she told me, when we have a home, "I would like to run an orphanage to help homeless children." I said "no", I do not think an orphanage will be part of our ministry. The reason I said that is because, I didn't like the way orphanages were being ran in Haiti. For example, they would raise the children from early childhood to 18 years old and then return them right back into the streets often to become unwed mothers. After we got married, she continued to share the orphanage dream of her heart and my answer was the same; eventually she stopped talking about it.

THE MIRACLE OF THE GIRLS HOME

In 1980 Hurricane Allen swept through Haiti causing devastating flooding and resultant mudslides which killed hundreds in the towns of St. Jean-du-Sud (South department) of Haiti. I called on my pastors association to collect funds and purchase food and medical supplies in order to bring relief to the Hurricane victims. We collected enough money to buy supplies to fill up a big semi truck with them. Renting a truck, a few pastors and I traveled 6 hours away from Port-Au-Prince to distribute the relief items. During the distribution, a heart breaking scene hit me. I saw many children being stepped on by adults who were fighting to get the relief provisions. I inquired about the children and found out they were mostly orphans of the Hurricane. Completing the distribution we returned to Port-Au-Prince, but these kids remained on my mind and it was difficult to sleep.

We collected additional funds, bought more food and supplies. Two weeks later we returned to the site of devastation for another distribution. This time it was even more heart breaking to see little 3 year old girls, in rags, dirty and fighting to gather some beans that had fallen on the ground.

I heard a voice telling me in repetitiously, "What would Jesus do? What would Jesus do? What would Jesus do?" I tried to dismiss that voice until we completed the distribution, and hopped in the truck to return to Port au Prince. The truck started up but the voice implored me," Save the lives of some of these children. Do not leave them. Do not let them down.

Do not let them die." I asked the driver to stop and I jumped out and ran to ask the adults to tell me whose children these were?" They replied there was no one of their families left to help them. I realized they would die if I did not help. I found a number of homeless orphaned girls wandering, in shock, among the devastation; their parents having been swept away by the deluge. I rescued 15 little girls and took them with me back home. These girls were sick, hungry, dirty and scared. Some of them were coughing badly. I prayed that they would survive the long and arduous journey to safety.

Bishop Joel rescued and brought home many frightened and life challenged Orphans of Hurricane Allen

DORIS HAD AN INSTANT ORPHANAGE!

Upon arriving back home my wife Doris came out to greet us and was surprised, when she saw the children disembarking from the truck. She asked me: "who are these children and where are you taking them? "Remembering her dream and earlier desire to run an orphanage; I replied, "Here are some girls for the orphanage you desired before and after we got married." She retorted, "You rejected my request for so many years until I stopped talking about it. I am not ready, take these girls back where you found them." We argued back and forth. My response was, "You asked for an orphanage, so here it is." Hers was, "You always said you didn't want to get involved with an orphanage, I am not ready for one right now." To end the argument, I left her, alone with the girls, for more than an hour.

When I returned the children were eating and she was cutting sheets to make some dresses to clothe them with. We had four very young sons but no garments for girls.

This certainly was a very big leap of faith. We were unprepared, with inadequate provisions, and no promises of help from anybody. God miraculously started opening doors. 'Gospel Crusade' gave us some bunk beds from their recently closed orphanage. Brother R.W Schambach brought us more beds and began supporting our new orphanage with donations for food.

More orphan girls discovering hope at their new home

A few months after we started the Home for the Girls; I was speaking at Christian Retreat Gospel Crusade in Bradenton, Florida. I was spoke about worry free living and mentioned the needs of our new girls' home and how we were depending on God to miraculously provide for them. After the service a dear sister approached me with a check for one thousand dollars. This was our first donation. Later on we became acquainted with our new donor; Mary Tobias and her husband Jim from Lyons, Kansas.

A few months later they come to Haiti and brought, sheets, clothing, towels and everything the girls had need of. They invited my wife and me to their home town in Kansas where we met their family and friends; the purpose of this visit was to explore the most effective way to support the orphanage.

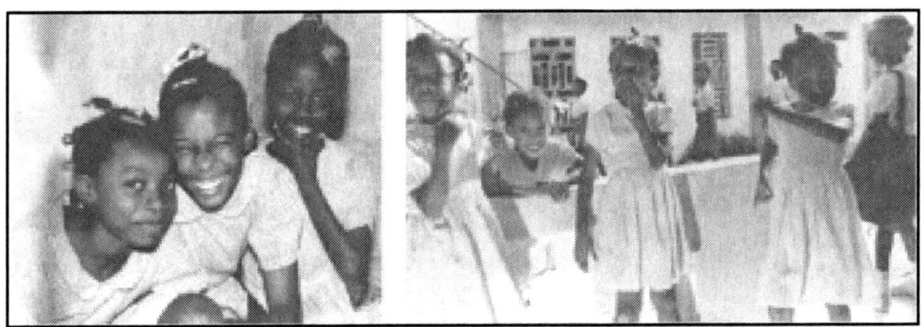

Out of sorrowful sadness springs joyful new life

Sitting with them in their living room, we formed a corporation that we named 'Haiti Love and Faith Ministries'. Soon, doctors, farmers and other concerned citizens, joined the cause and were able to raise enough money to contribute toward purchasing land and building a very nice home, for the girls, at Lamentin in Carrefour.

This was just the beginning of a long succession of children, both boys and girls, whom we would rescue from dire circumstances. Many of their parents were infected with HIV/Aids, Tuberculosis, Malaria and other diseases; often dying violent deaths in the poverty stricken maelstrom which has defined Haiti as the poorest country in the Western Hemisphere. These orphaned children were left to become wandering waifs.

One child led to another and before long our home was overflowing with children so we opened up another building as a boys' home. Eventually the girls, now numbering 55, got their own home adjacent to our church on Rue Lamentin in Carrefour.

God Blessed us with one of the nicest Homes in Haiti for Girls

THE MIRACLE OF THE BOYS HOME

We had no vision or plan to start or run a boys' home in parallel with the girls home, our load already being too heavy; but God had other plans.

Here is how it came about: Virginia Louis, an American missionary lady had established and operated an orphanage for both boys and girls for many years in Carrefour. It became urgently necessary for her to leave Haiti and she asked my wife and me to consider taking the children into our new orphanage. We said "NO!" We had no room, no means and we never accepted the idea of mixing boys and girls together. At her insistence, with only three days to decide, we went on our knees, crying out to God. He answered: "Take them, I will provide."

She left the children in their rented house under our care; we moved her girls to our girls' home and kept the boys in that same rented house for about six months.

We shared the Boys Home vision with our good friend Bill Moore who ran an organization named Evangelical Family

Services (EFS), who helped put a support committee together in Telford Pennsylvania with members from Grace Chapel Missions, Branch Creek Fellowship, Bill Hooper, Clint and Leanne Miller, Pastor Lee Miller and others to handle the sponsorship and building program for the boys.

After a couple of years they helped raise the funds to purchase the property and build a home, for the boys, next door to our church property. Today, many of the boys have gone on to Bible colleges in Christ For the Nations Institute and other Schools in Haiti, Canada and United States; some are married and living a good life. All the Glory goes to God!

Joel and Doris Jeune at the Boys orphanage in earlier days

The boys' home remains where it began on Waney Street, where our original church and now, also, school, library and widows home are located, all in Carrefour, Port Au Prince. All the boys and girls go to school and are fed and clothed the best we can provide.

Our extended family of children arrives from the mean streets of homelessness but with God's nurturing grace, the support of their North American sponsors and our faithful partners; they grow up spiritually, physically and emotionally healthy.

Our Family continued to Grow

Our youth move on to high school and many graduate on to advanced education such as nursing, accounting, home economics, business and medical schools; becoming professionals in a variety of fields. Some move on to be school teachers, administrators; even pastors in our, or other, churches.

Graduated from Bible School, with some boys, at the home he grew up in

After graduating from college, Edline married a good Christian and both she and her husband are bank managers.

GRACE HAITI PEDIATRIC HOSPITAL

Many of our original 15 girls were sick, requiring us to make numerous trips each week to existing medical centers where health care was often unreliable. Working with children for so long we realized how desperately the little ones needed medical help; for there is so much sickness attacking them.

We realized the eventual need for a medical clinic of our own. From this reality would spring the larger vision of a dedicated pediatric hospital in Haiti.

The Lord convicted our hearts and for many years gave us a vision to build a Pediatric Hospital.

Miraculously, the Lord provided us with the land that was needed through contributions from God's people. God has imparted that same vision to some others; especially, the late Sister Dorothy Cooper of Bradenton Florida who willed a large memorial gift, Brother Dick and Sister Joyce Helman (Snowden).

THE RAGLAND'S OUTSTANDING CONTRIBUTIONS

Bishop Joel and Reverends George and Barbara Ragland with Doris Jeune

Reverends George & Barbara Ragland of Wings of Victory International out of St. Petersburg, Florida worked, with us, for 4 years on the plans, architectural drawings and renderings: along with Engineering Ministries International (EMI), they worked on the engineering & technical plans for both the Medical/Missionary Guesthouse as well as the Grace Haiti Pediatric Hospital. They were also involved in many other aspects of the project such as fundraising & project development and contributed significantly of their personal finances.

Dick and Joyce Helman of Good News In Action Ministries contributed significant support to the successful planning of our medical facilities.

Sister Jan Crouch of Trinity Broadcasting Network and Smile of a Child rallied her viewing audience to contribute finances toward the construction costs. Gospel Crusade funded our hospital project significantly, as did many others.

There was a completed, and frequently used, medical residence for the visiting doctors and nurses to stay in when they came to work and teach advanced techniques at our walk in clinic. This residence was destroyed in the earthquake but a new and better, seismically resistant one, will (and must) be built as funds become available to do so.

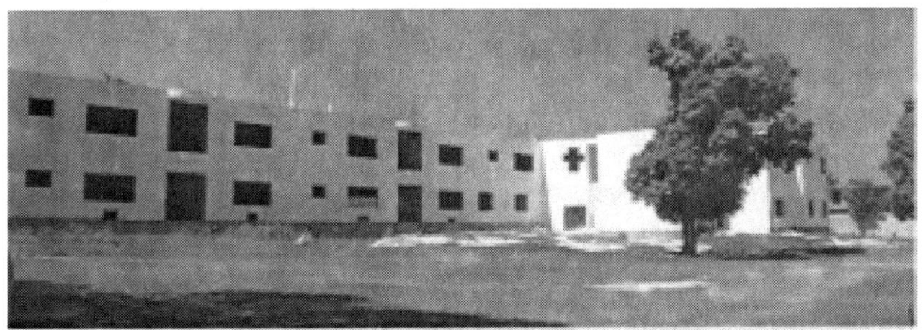

The Beautiful 2 story Grace Haiti Pediatric Hospital

The 130-bed hospital, when completed as a pediatric center, will have operating rooms, laboratory, x-ray and other diagnostic facilities and much more. This will be a high-tech hospital. People will come from all over the country for treatments they cannot find elsewhere. We will treat and heal children to begin with. Later on, we might include geriatric treatment for the elderly.

Consider supporting this special children's ministry, which started, heartfelt and humble, by taking in 15 child survivors of a terrible storm. We met the need, on the hurricane ravaged ground, where it was; just as Jesus always did and how he taught us in the parable of the "Good Samaritan".

Dr. Mary Mica Desir and others, who were raised and nurtured in our boys' and girls' homes, have gone on to be licensed doctors and nurses and have served the public in our medical clinic and elsewhere for many years. Dr. Mica also worked with Doctors without Borders at our Pediatric Hospital during their year's tenure of turning it into a general hospital after the 2010 earthquake.

The fruits of our labors are evident in the accomplishments of those whom we've rescued from humble backgrounds and humiliating areas of our Haitian society and raised up to be fine young men and women who will be the brighter future of our homeland.

My most gratifying accomplishment has been raising our youngsters in the teachings of the Bible, within the nurturing confines of the church; so that many of them are actively serving God's people in many capacities including pastoring in or even establishing new churches. A significant part of my success has been spiritual mentoring of the young men and women God has placed in my stead. They are my successors and are, as they go out on their own, reproducing what God taught me and I in turn passed on to them. God is using them as He has used me since He raised me from the valley of the shadow of death. Some of them might have died had God not placed them in our care, but praise the Lord, they live and are blessing their families and communities with Godly service. I thank God to have been a part of His great work in these young Haitians lives.

I have a mandate from God to save the whole nation; to escort all nine million Haitians to heaven. Whatever I accomplish, no matter where I do it; my bottom line is to save peoples' souls and establish God's kingdom. I do what I do because there are many more people who need to accept and be embraced by God. I will keep the Faith and keep on going until I can do it no more.

I have many goals that have not yet been met. I've always had a heart for children. It is fulfilling to experience God's blessings raining down upon our Children's Ministry, the Feeding Program, Orphanages and the Children's Hospital.

We welcome you to come to Haiti and see the fruits of what God is doing right now through Grace International, Inc. and Gospel Crusade of Haiti. All Glory goes to our great and loving God.

When you give donations to our ministry your gifts go 100% to the work of God. Giving to our ministry is sowing into good soil. God always blesses people who do. Our ministry keeps good records with full transparency and complete accountability. All gifts and donations made to Grace International, Inc. are tax-deductible.

Bishop Jeune, chief contractor Bielinois Antoine, supervising engineer Reynold Gousse at Grace Haiti Pediatric Hospital

Widows' Home

I also have a heart for the elderly and I've been called to start an Elderly Widows Home because in Haiti the elderly usually live in pitiful circumstances during their twilight years. There is no societal help for them; no government assistance program. We are the first church, as far as I know, that has opened and is maintaining a widow's home with a number of sweet senior citizens in residence. This is another one of the goals that is being fulfilled in my lifetime. Within the past decade we've provided a Widow's Home for those elderly women less fortunate than others or who have no family to care for them. About 20 widows have been sheltered, encouraged and helped to feel at home through this facility. We give a special thank you to Christian Retreat and Gospel Crusade of Florida and to Dr. Patricia Bailey-Jones of Master's Touch Ministries for their vital contribution to the building of a beautiful home for these precious elderly widows.

The Lord called us to build an elderly widows home

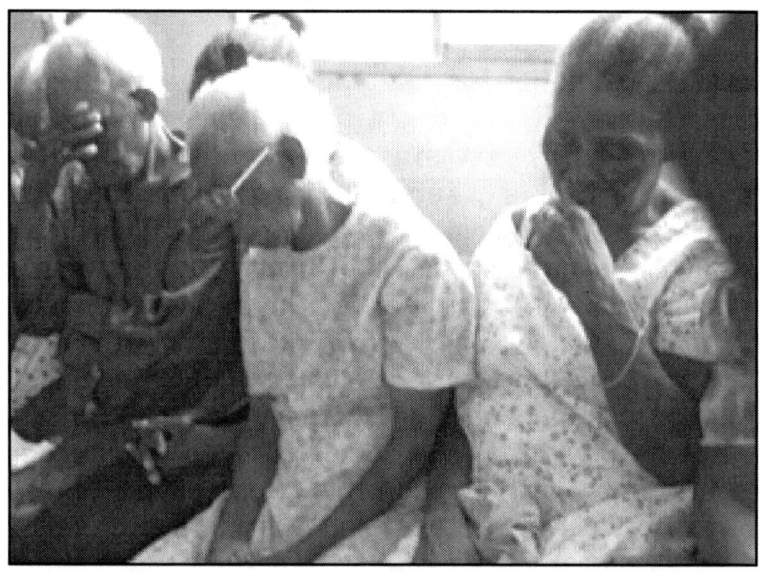

Prayer is a part of the widows' daily life

FEEDING THE CHILDREN

Children have been a vital part of our ministry from its inception. A few months after we started our little school we realized that we needed to feed them. Many of their parents were unable to feed them before they went to school. The boys and girls were hungry and sleeping in class, finding it difficult to concentrate, past their growling tummies', and to study.

We went to our knees before the Lord in prayer and commenced fasting. We exhorted our new church members to also pray for the children's needs to be met.

On one of his visits to Haiti, Dr. Luke Weaver, the pastor of Grace Chapel Mission in Pennsylvania brought some candy to distribute to the children and was profoundly moved seeing how hungry they were. Upon returning home, he made up contribution cards requesting his congregation to support a children's' feeding program in Haiti. With this first support we began the school feeding program that endures to this day.

Other churches, ministries and individuals also caught the vision and extended their faithful support for many years.

Gospel Crusade of Haiti also established many feeding centers in their church schools all around Haiti.

The feeding program that we conduct for the children is divided into four sections aimed at different groups of children.

Children in the orphanages are fed three times daily and have a safe, secure home to live in. We provide the education and the love, etc., everything they need to make this a family home for them.

The second feeding program is at our school where the attendees eat a nutritious lunch; which for many of them is the one and only meal they can count on each day.

The third program feeds the street children and others who are also welcome to partake and participate. Additionally, every summer for three months, six days a week, we include a Bible study (Summer Bible School) opportunity for participants to learn about and to worship God.

Feeding the school children helps them stay happy and ready to learn.

Bishop Jeune ministering to the children

THE LORD'S KITCHEN

The newest feeding program addresses the hovering hunger of the multitude of homeless children encamped at Grace Village. Since Easter of 2010, we have been operating The Lord's Kitchen feeding program for the refugee population inhabiting our compound at 54 Lamentin in Carrefour, Haiti.

Several weeks before Easter Pastor Doris and I were thinking of a way to make it a special blessing for our refugee campers. We felt led by God to serve a special, one time, Resurrection Sunday meal to the hurting and hungry. God expanded that vision into an ongoing daily ministry to feed and minister the love of Jesus to the multitudes forced, by the cataclysm, from their fallen homes into the safe haven of our blessed Grace Village.

We shared this vision with many other churches and groups and extended an invitation for them to participate in supporting the Lord's Kitchen. Some of them seized the opportunity and sent their members to our refugee camp to help cook and distribute hundreds of meals each day to the children. The little Orphans of the Storm stand in line, waiting with bowls in hand, to be filled with a nutritious hot meal; which they take back to their makeshift tent and tarp shelters and share with their families.

We thank God for His provision. Sadly we have occasionally gone a week or two without available food resources; unable to feed the children. By His grace the Lord's kitchen always resumes and continues to bless both those receiving as well as those serving.

More information is available to anyone who would like the opportunity to participate and be a blessing to the children.

Call Jerri at our Miami Gardens office at 305-231-1117 or E mail us at office@graceintl.org.

Bishop Jeune with Earthquake Survivor Children at Grace Village, Lord's Kitchen Feeding Program

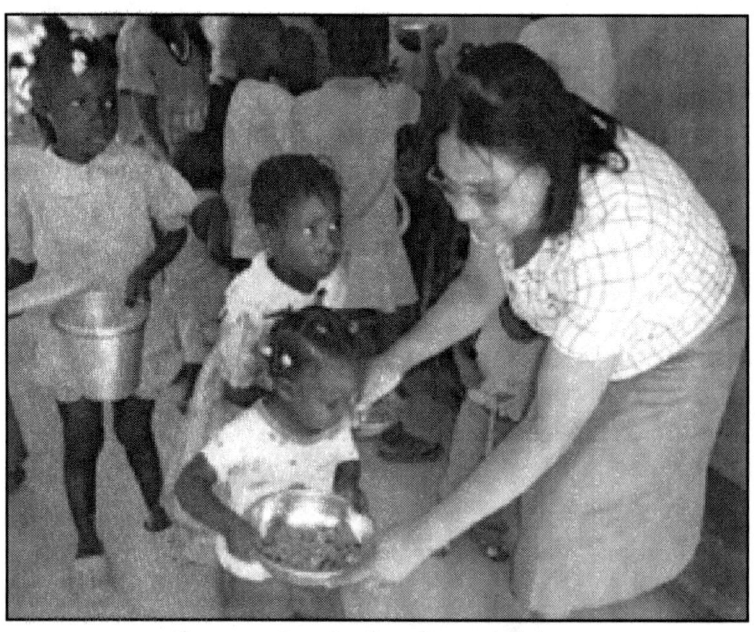

Mommy Doris feeding children

Children waiting for God's blessed food

Church Teams come to help feed the children

CHAPTER 13

Haiti Children's Christmas

By Marlon Migala

Christmas is a special time for all of Christendom but its celebration is, usually, not nearly as humble as what is experienced in Haiti.

Once upon a time a little girl nicknamed "Guerly" was, like so many Haitian children, growing up in an orphanage. She had to share everything with her fellow orphans and slept with her shoes on or tucked under her pillow lest another child should appropriate them away from her in the night.

Haitian orphanages, operating on modest budgets, provide basic food as available and shelter for their children but not much more. They rely on the goodwill of friends and partners in other lands; mostly in North America and largely from Christian organizations. Care packages with clothing and treats are sent from churches and individuals who also, often, sponsor one or more of the children with monthly monetary commitments.

Like many Haitian children, Guerly was born to parents who were not able to keep and raise her; so they gave her up for adoption, when she was just five days old, to a Jamaican lady named Doris Burke. Guerly, now named Doris L Burke, went to live in the orphanage home run by Mrs. Burke. At the orphanage; a candy bar, box of raisins or bottle of soda was shared, often by a dozen or more children. Each would taste a sliver, a morsel or a sip; a fleeting treat in a land of need.

An extraordinary Christmas time happened one year for Guerly and thousands of other orphaned boys and girls who were bused to and filled a soccer stadium in Port au-Prince. It would become a seminal day in the life of young Doris "Guerly" Burke.

An American evangelist named Nick Grewick rented the largest venue available and, with his team, staged a day of Joy for the multitudes of little ones, most of whom had never experienced anything at all like it. There was music, puppets, song time audience participation and child friendly entertainment. There were individual bags of pate, sweet treat goodies and each child had their own soda. This was truly a Papa Nick come to bless all with a day to remember. He returned with his Christmas outreach team many times and Guerly would remember those special days. She would incorporate the example of those altruistic loving kindnesses into her world vision. Those days of joy would inform her thinking up to the present time.

Marlon and Jerri Migala met Pastor Doris and Bishop Jeune while Jerri was working for Trinity Broadcasting Network and Marlon, a poet, playwright, essayist and wordsmith, was producing theatre, featuring puppets. Jerri began assisting Doris in arranging a feeding program for her orphanage and thousands of school children in Carrefour. She listened to Doris' recollections about those pleasant days of yore when Evangelist Nick would gather together those childhood dreamers and gift them with a day of sweet substance each year.

Doris' fond memories impressed themselves on Jerri who, upon hearing about them, was led to encourage her to fulfill the vision of creating a Christmas time, for others, reminiscent of the ones that had sustained her childhood hopes.

Doris received repeated positive feedback from the children of Haiti and requests for the puppet characters they had seen on the 'Haitian Praise The Lord' television program to come visit and perform a live show for them. She thought; why not create a Christmas program, featuring puppets, depicting the story of the birth of Jesus. She enlisted Marlon and Jerri to help and they built giant puppets characterizing Joseph, Mary, the Shepherds, Wisemen and an Innkeeper with his hotel and stable, a Bethlehem town gossip and, of course, a baby Jesus. Puppets and props were constructed at Marlon's studio in North Miami Beach, Florida and then partially disassembled to be packed in cases for air travel to Haiti. A donkey costume was made for two boys to wear and for the Joseph and Mary puppets to ride on from Nazareth to Bethlehem. Lamb ears for little boys to wear were sewn. An angel costume with wings, shepherds attire and 'JoJo', the dog, full body puppet costume were borrowed from Words of Life Fellowship Church. Five thousand dolls and trucks were donated from various sources and Words of Life provided 10,000 balloons with "Jesus Loves You" in various languages imprinted on them. These balloons had, for many previous years, already been a joyful evangelistic gift from Jerri Migala's Balloons International to many churches and missionaries.

Pastor Doris Jeune is a great organizer and she arranged for 5,000 boys and girls from many schools and orphanages, as well as Grace's own children, along with others from a handicapped childrens' home, to be bused to the National Theater of Haiti in downtown Port-au—Prince. Each child would partake of a pate snack with sweet treats, popcorn and a balloon in a lunch bag along with a fruit juice. "Jesus Loves You" balloon's festooned an auditorium decorated by dozens of helpers. All night before the party, a production team popped corn and prepared thousands of bags filled with toys and goodies.

The day before the Christmas Party, Doris along with Marlon, Jerri and Sunjoy Walters, a sister from Words of Life, rehearsed the production with their volunteer team. The cast of performers was made up of Haitian youth and children, recruited from Grace's orphanages and Tabernacle De La Grace Church. They would carry and manipulate the giant puppets (Pageant Style).

The stage was Broadway Theater large and had often been performed on by the National Ballet of Haiti. No stage lights or electricity were available but sunlight softly filtered through a translucent roof creating a pleasantly perfect golden glow.

A gas powered generator powered up our sound system. The team was thrilled at all the space on which to choreograph the puppet movements. Some of the Nativity Puppets would enter from the stage wings while others would come down the aisles from the top rows of the stadium style seating. The sight lines were excellent from all of the bench seats even at the top of the auditorium. We were all happy with anticipation!

Roosters, mooing cows and bleating goats sound the wake up calls in Haiti. Marlon and Jerri were driven to Michael Jeune's High School in Delmas in order to get him furloughed for the day in exchange for a short puppet show performed for the high school classes.

Upon our arrival at the National Theater, we discovered that all the seating and half of the stage along with all the isles were fully occupied with children. All the choreography had to be changed and improvised on the spot. More than five thousand children's voices were enthusiastically resonating throughout the theatre with an energetic buzz.

Judith Legale from Grace Girls Home was our translator. Brother Damas Morency, from Grace Tabernacle De La Grace Church, was the Master of Ceremonies, for this first performance and party, as he would continue to be every year that followed. He warmed up the audience with songs of praise that raised the roof for Jesus. The atmosphere was charged with great excitement and anticipation of what was about to happen. Thousands of children would remember this day for the rest of their lives. We didn't know it, at the time, but this day would be a harbinger of celebrations in years to come.

Our faithful Haitian actor, Guetenberg "Guerber" Baptiste joyfully romped throughout the audience dressed as JoJo; the playful dog character well known and loved by many in the audience who had seen him in our children's program videos. The children chanted "JoJo, JoJo", welcoming his entrance and he imparted great gladness and laughter to them. Later "Guerber" was a Bethlehem shepherd leading some little boy actors, playing his lambs, bleating BAA . . . BAA's as they made their vocally amusing entrance on to the stage during the first scene of our Christmas Play.

The Christmas Puppet play, that I had written, opened with Luce Andral, as the Angel, announcing God's blessed intent to Mary. Luce, as the angel, has continued to grace every stage in every year since then. About twenty Haitian youth were involved in the Christmas puppet show.

In the years that followed, our Christmas Party celebration of Jesus Birth would travel to many locations. Performances at schools and college auditoriums, open air plazas, orphanage courtyards, and a boys' detention center in the greater Port-au-Prince area, Delmas, Petionville and Carrefour would bring joy to the children of the future of Haiti.

In recent years we were joined by Ed and Kathy Keith, Paulette Cheeks and many other helping hands including Pastors' Mark Jones and Chris Connell along with their men and women from the Raleigh First Assembly of God, Raleigh North Carolina. Pastor Eric Jarvis from First Assembly of God, South Haven, Michigan also joined our Christmas team.

Pastor Doris' vision, born of "Guerly's" hopes and dreams; inspired by Evangelist Nick's Christmas outreach would grow even brighter. Beginning at the National Theatre, circa 1997, thousands of children have received Jesus as their Lord and Savior, during the ensuing years.

One year, with more than ten thousand in attendance, nearly 7,000 decided to follow Jesus, the other 3,000 had already done so before. That same year with only 8,000 officially expected, via RSVP, another 2,000 unexpectedly arrived. Pastor Doris' kitchens had prepared enough food for 8,000 but, in a 'Loaves and Fishes' miracle, God multiplied the food and all were fed a chicken, salad, rice and beans dinner.

For a few years the Samaritan's Purse's Operation Christmas Child gift boxes blessed the children but one year the customs officials, impounded one of the containers with 10,000 gift laden shoe boxes inside. The ransom for those gifts was so great that it took one year to collect sufficient funds to pay for the container to be released.

American Airlines had graciously flown our toy gifts at no charge, providing humanitarian relief labels, with their logo, to affix upon our packages of toys and baggage. Great thanks go to our friends at American Airlines for their assistance over the years in flying thousands of toys and party supplies to Haiti each year. We gratefully thank Annie Griffin our joy toy courier, Marva King and employees of American Airlines, for all of their assistance.

One year there were 60 boxes of donated toys that Marlon and Jerri, with a little help from their friends, packed up in their garage. These gifts and toys were donated from Grace Partners all around America.

Arriving at the Port-au-Prince airport Pastor Doris was challenged by the customs officials who wanted to impound the toys until a ransom would be paid. This was unacceptable! Grace had not collected these toys that would bring joy to Haiti's children to have customs deny them their gifts or charge exorbitant tariffs for these gifts to be freely given.

Doris and the Fourteen Christmas Missionaries from the USA formed a circle, in the now deserted terminal, calling out for God to intervene and release the gift boxes. Apparently the fear of the Lord descended upon the airport officials because the chief of customs approached Doris telling her to "take your boxes and go, you are free to leave!" No tariff on the toys was charged and he even ordered his men to help remove the boxes safely to the waiting buses. God had once again prevailed and moved this troublesome mountain out of the way.

Guerber, as "JoJo", Welcomes Thousands of Children to the Christmas Party

GODS MIRACLE OF MULTIPLICATION

God has multiplied the gift toys every year but one of the most miraculous times, was when a container of toys was delayed by customs and children who had been at the Christmas party all day waited until nightfall for their gifts. Pastor Doris went to a small closet containing a few bags of about 1,000 dolls and trucks, praying along with the team that God would multiply these toys for the six thousand patiently waiting children. They took the bags of toys and began distributing them and low and behold every child went home fulfilled with a toy. The tired but joyous team was in awe of this latest miracle from God.

One year the Christmas team went to share the Joy of Jesus birth bringing festive balloons, puppets, hamburgers and other goodies only to be turned away by the Boys Detention home administration.

The boys crowded around us begging for clean water, their lips were parched white and cracked from thirst. They took us to a hole in the ground showing us how they would dip a can to draw out the green polluted water to drink. We were stunned!

Often children had begged us for food. This was the first time children were begging us for water. Pastor Doris resolved with God's help to rectify this situation. Along with generous partners (BD foundation, Connie Klein and her family) a clean water well was built for the 600 boys at the center. The next Christmas we were welcomed to bring a full Christmas party with a puppet show and gifts to the Boys Detention home.

Pastors Chris Connell and Mark Jones from First Assembly of God, Raleigh, North Carolina and their team performed our Christmas show with Marlon's International Puppets for the 600 boys, most of whom accepted Jesus as their personal Lord and Savior. Church women from Tabernacle De La Grace Church cooked a wonderful dinner for all and toys were distributed to every boy and girl.

A TIME OF LOAVES AND FISHES

In 2010 the year of the great earthquake we were able to obtain Operation Christmas Child gift filled shoe boxes from Samaritan's Purse once again but while promised 10,000 we only received 2,000. We decided to distribute them at the largest venue on our performance tour. The gymnasium in downtown Port Au Prince had sustained some damage and its parking lot was, like most outdoor open spaces, filled with tents and tarps.

We performed our Christmas show to some 3,500 children sitting in balcony bleachers on either side of the basketball court. The sound system repeatedly malfunctioned and a variety of other distractions challenged our perseverance and patience but we soldiered on and completed our show.

We had more than a dozen volunteers from Fuller and Forward Edge who were in Haiti constructing homes with Grace at our Lambi development site joining us this day to distribute the shoebox gifts. They along with Grace Team members and our all Haitian puppet team formed two lines between which the children filed through receiving their gifts as they went, from our smiling Samaritans, on their way to exit the gym.

With more than a thousand children still in the bleachers Marlon did a count of the remaining gift boxes and found around 400 left; not nearly enough to go around and yet every child got a gift box. Another 'Loaves and Fishes' miracle had taken place.

This evangelistic outreach, toys, food treats and the special joy that the Christmas program has brought to tens of thousands of children are an annual fulfillment of "Guerly's" dream. She is recreating her childhood's special Christmas times for the present day boys and girls of Haiti's Orphans of the Storm who, after the great earthquake of January 2010, are living in a Sea of Sorrows. The parties are bringing hope to the children of Haiti.

We are thankful to all who have made these parties possible, especially Pastor Stanley Moore and Words of Life Church, who have supported these parties for many years.

In the years to come, as Haiti is reconstructed out of the ashes and rubble of the earthquake disaster, its children will need to have times of joy and laughter to relieve their sorrows. We, at Grace International and Grace Village in Haiti, welcome your support in making the continuation of joyful events for these precious children happen. Please refer to the contact information at the end of this book.

Joy unspeakable at Christmas Parties

CHAPTER 14

Rescue, Relief And Restoration

By Marlon Migala and Jonny Jeune

RESCUE

The earthquake of January 12, 2010 will be remembered by all Haitians who were there that awful day as well as all of us who care for Haiti and its people. When the earth shook it destroyed tens of thousands of structures, killing 300,000 people, leaving more than a million homeless. Tremors of death and despair were felt around the world.

On that fateful day we all became Haitians. The bell tolled for all of us. How sad, that it often takes great tragedy to foster greater unity among all of God's people.

The first responders sped to the woe beset island nation to search for any survivors in a Sea of Sorrows spawned by a cataclysm that struck an already fragile democracy.

Once upon a time Haiti was the birthplace (in modern times) of liberation from slavery; a gift of courage and solidarity to the world at large and to the America's.

RELIEF

Now, we bend to the task of rescuing the crippled in body; healing the wounds, relieving the pain and restoring the traumatized minds of the innocent children, the grown and the elderly. We rush to provide good, safe water and nourishing food sustenance to halt the spread of disease and starvation in a nation already living perilously involved with these calamities.

In partnership with the World Food Program, Grace Village has been the distribution center for food to over 100,000 people in the Carrefour area.

A program has been established to allow Haitian children to travel to the United States and receive life-saving surgery or special medical procedures unavailable to them in Haitian hospitals.

Though our guest house has been destroyed; our school, church and orphanage structures damaged; we are, none-the-less, a safe haven for more than 20,000 homeless refugees of the seismic terror. We have become a safe space; a safe harbor in a Sea of Sorrows. Our decades old reputation of peace, love and charity has, like a spiritual magnet, drawn the pilgrims of this latest disaster into our walled oasis in the desert of desolation.

GRACE VILLAGE A REFUGEE CAMP FROM CHAOS

The home base of Grace International's work in Haiti is Grace Village, a 20-acre compound located in Carrefour, a county just West of Port-au-Prince. Prior to the earthquake, Carrefour was already one of the more demoralizing parts of the Western section of Haiti. The living conditions were the most precarious. The unemployment rate was in excess of 90% with very few economic or cultural activities in the area to improve the living conditions. The population of 450,000 exceeded the ability of local municipal services to support their needs.

The internationally acclaimed, Doctors Without Borders recognized our positive impact on and well respected standing among the Haitian citizenry both in our home city of Carrefour as well as Port au Prince and beyond. Our profile as a Christian NGO (Non Governmental Organization) in and for the Haitian community is well known by many in North America and the Caribbean.

With foresight we built a hospital, originally intended for children, to the highest, most stringent standards and specifications to be earthquake resistant; and it was. While other buildings crumbled and fell into concrete and cinderblock rubble; our hospital stood strong, with no more than a little cosmetic blemish; indicating that the epicenter of the tectonic chaos occurring in the earth's crust below it had changed the face of Haiti.

Doctors Without Borders came forth to partner with us at Grace International; occupying and staffing our hospital as a medical relief facility, after the earthquake, for all in need of their Hippocratic oath commitment. Our hospital has been the largest medical facility used by them in all of Haiti.

Someday it will be a preeminent children's hospital for all of Haiti with the best and most modern healing methodologies as well as a receptacle of God's healing power through His people's prayers and healing hands. Now our building that defied the quake is taking in the injured, sick and wounded that they might live and not die.

Teams of volunteer medical personnel are rotating into our campuses at Lamentin 54 and Waney 93 to assist with this most massive relief effort in the annals of Haiti.

Arise and Walk Ministries Foundation under the leadership of Doctor Mark Wade maintained a constant and consistent Samaritan presence at our compounds.

The thousands of displaced persons who streamed into our compounds, especially the larger 20 acre Grace Village, have created a makeshift temporary town of tents, tarps, sheets and saplings. They are, however, sleeping at ground level and the yearly rainy season with its potential of rapid flooding and destructive storms challenges all in a deforested, ecologically damaged country.

Despite these unprecedented challenges, the staff at Grace Village has organized our compound into an example of proactive, healthy, and efficient camp management; that has been surveyed, studied and emulated by organizations in other camps.

Our camp has been organized into sectioned blocks each of which is represented by a block captain and a small committee. Water wells, showers, toilets, and a trash disposal system have been implemented to prevent the many health risks typically associated with such situations.

Those walls surrounding Grace Village, which were damaged by the earthquake, have been rebuilt and security personnel patrol the compound to ensure the best possible civil safety.

Grace Village Tent City after the 2010 Earthquake

RESTORATION and EMPOWERMENT

Toward the goal of restoring our weary post earthquake pilgrims to normal, healthy lives; we have drawn up architecturally designed plans for a new Grace Village. Now under construction on land we have acquired at Lambi in Greccier County, homes of various sizes built by volunteer teams and, with their own sweat equity, by the intended recipients.

These homes will be ecologically viable with solar, photo-voltaic, electrification and modern sanitation facilities such as composting toilets. There will be clean and grey water collection, storage and recycling. Many low tech, green technologies designed to help create a sustainable future life style for Haiti will be implemented.

Garden and foliage abundant spaces will replace the hard scrabble wastelands of a long misused and neglected landscape once known as the 'Pearl of the Antilles'.

New, well appointed schools, clinics, recreational and church structures will serve the common good. Educational, job skills training as well as industries to create meaningful employment will empower the people to produce life affirming abundance for the common good.

These homes, community structures, as well as fostering spiritual well being are all part of Grace International's commitment for the future of a new and better Haiti.

You, dear reader, can join with us in this exciting opportunity to build something new and wonderful rising out of the ashes of a tragedy of epic proportions.

We are looking for Pioneers of a New and Better Haiti. Will you be one of those Pioneers who will help us break new ground, reach out to new horizons and help write a new chapter in Haiti's history?

You can be part of a new liberation movement of freedom from poverty, fear, poor health and disease. You can help create a model community for the children to grow up in and their parents to work productively in; a community that shall inspire all of Haiti.

You can help build an ecologically profound, environmentally sustainable village: a new town for a new Haiti; with hurricane and earthquake resistant homes, a village with schools, a community center and park, playgrounds for children a soccer football field and other recreational facilities.

A village where dreams can come true; where entrepreneur opportunities abound and are supported by architectural and technologically progressive innovations; where industries to employ its citizens will build their factories and facilities.

This will be a village whose interior and outskirts will become verdant with garden farming and fruit bearing trees; a place of personal and communal empowerment.

A place where true democracy of, by and for the people can be realized to show the rest of Haiti and the world what

God can do through the creative talents, hearts and minds of the real Haitian people.

EMPOWERMENT PROGRAM FOR A NEW HAITI

by Jonny Jeune

Tent City at Grace Village next to our Hospital

Grace International's **Haiti Empowerment Program** is off the drawing board and into action. We have broken ground toward material and social development. Our goal is to pioneer in the creation of a new Haiti.

Location of our Lambi Community Development

Our **Haiti Empowerment Program** is progressing well. Although this program started a couple of years prior to the earthquake, challenges arising from the effects spawned by the earthquake have motivated us to proceed with urgency.

There are four main categories that are currently part of this process. Additional partnerships are being finalized for the advancement of these projects. However we welcome and are open to new partners who will understand and subscribe to Grace's vision for this New Haiti.

The **Haiti Empowerment Program** encompasses several projects bringing relief and restoring to normal, healthy lives the thousands of displaced survivors of the earthquake as well as those who were already living in dire circumstances and abject poverty. Our program's main goal is to create economic opportunities and much better living conditions thus freeing the people we serve from the chains of poverty's bondage.

Under construction is our current project, The **Lambi Community** Partnership for Sustainable Living.

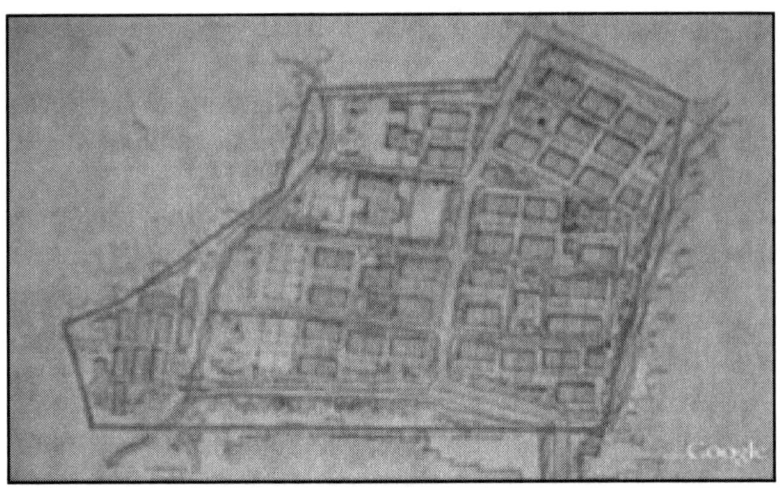

Lambi community site plan

Agribusiness—Current Partners: Forward Edge and Jamaican Broilers Group (to create and promote chicken-farming). Project Budget: Available upon request.

Housing—Current Partners: Fuller Center, Forward Edge and Engineering Ministries International: community building via permanent housing solutions. Project Budget: Available upon request.

Alternative Energy—Current Partner: GAIA: producing bio-fuel products for cooking; and eventually fueling retrofitted vehicles from petrol to ethanol and providing ethanol cook stoves to our Haitian communities. Project Budget: Available upon request.

Business Training & Opportunities—Current Partner: Project Eden: educating business owners in better business development, improving job skills for construction related tradesmen and teaching individual entrepreneurs basic business practices. Annual Budget: Available upon request.

To get involved in all of these projects please go to our web site: www.graceintl.org or write to the address at the end of this book.

Update on our Progress

On Monday, November 22nd, 2010 we broke ground on our first sustainable community at Lambi, in Gressier County, Haiti. This 7 acre site will have 76 homes, a market area, community center and place of worship, a communal water well and bathrooms.

Since then Forward Edge and Solid Rock Church have constructed a number of transitional homes on the site and these dwellings are now occupied by families who lost their homes to the earthquake.

Fuller Center, augmented by and working with the intended recipients of the permanent stone constructed homes, has built several of them. These families, having demonstrated personal initiative by contributing their own sweat equity into the construction process, have moved into their new homes.

The earthquake survivors are thriving on the land at Lambi that God and His people have opened up for their new tomorrows.

This past July, Project Eden helped train 26 construction industry tradesmen and businessmen from Grace International's community. This group is part of the initial tradesmen building our new community at Lambi.

We thank our provider, Almighty God, for bringing us together to embark upon this pioneer effort for a new Haiti. We aim to glorify His name and to improve the lives of His people. We believe that the work in Haiti is in obedience to what Jesus commands. We look forward to your continued pioneering partnership with us in the development and implementation of this program.

SPIRITUAL MINISTRIES

270 Churches with Gospel Crusade, Inc.
Leadership Training
Pastoral Seminars
Bible Schools
TV-Radio Ministry
Youth Outreach
Sports Programs
Children's Church
Women's Conferences
Prayer Campaigns
Evangelism Mass Crusades
International Traveling and Teaching Ministries

SOCIAL AND HUMANITARIAN OUTREACHES

Daily Children's Feeding Programs
Food Bank for the Hungry
70 Christian Schools
3 Orphanages
Elderly Widow's Home
Medical and Dental Clinics
HIV Program
Grace Haiti Pediatric Hospital
Short Term Medical Missions

Short Term Ministry and Work Project Missions
Youth Vocational Training Programs
Christian Economic Revolution
English Language & Computer Schools

FUTURE PLANS AND VISION

Community (Micro-Financing) Development Bank
Environmental Restoration through Reforestation
Distribution of Alcohol/Ethanol Cook Stoves
Affordable Basic Utility Vehicle Distribution
Low Income and Homeless Housing Projects
Empowerment Programs
Building Sustainable Communities
Radio and Television Stations

GRACE INTERNATIONAL

Grace International, Inc. is a non-profit (501c3) organization registered in the State of Florida, with its main operations for nearly 40 years on the Island of Haiti and USA offices in Miami Gardens, Florida.

Our mission is to RESCUE, RELIEVE, and RESTORE by providing health-care, education, spiritual guidance, feeding programs, and empowered living to those, within our reach.

Operating since 1974, Grace International was founded by Bishop Joel and his wife Pastor Doris Jeune, who together oversee and lead the organization in the roles of President and Vice President.

For the past 40 years, Grace International has been impacting lives through the oversight and management of 270 churches, 70 plus Christian schools, 3 orphanages, as well as a medical clinic, a hospital and a home for elderly widows.

Within these programs and facilities, Grace International also operates feeding programs, various learning centers as well as seasonal and annual conferences.

The base of the organization's work in Haiti is Grace Village, located in the county of Carrefour, adjacent to the capital city of Port Au Prince.

After the earthquake, more than 25,000 people sought refuge and were provided a safe haven from their 'sea of sorrows' at Grace Village, transforming it into the second largest refugee camp in the greater Port Au Prince area. The epicenter of that seismic cataclysm was in our vicinity of Haiti.

Grace International is working to resettle the displaced pilgrims living in this camp and to create small communities that are models of healthy, holistic, sustainable and industrious living.

WHAT WE DO

Children from Grace Village

HEALTH
GRACE HAITI PEDIATRIC HOSPITAL

With the partnership of donors and supporters all over the world, we have built a hospital in Carrefour where people from all over Haiti are able to receive excellent medical care and services they would otherwise go without.

In 2010, we formed a partnership with Medecins Sans Frontiere, becoming the largest Medecins Sans Frontiers site in Haiti.

GRACE MEDICAL & DENTAL MOBILE CLINICS

Periodically, we send out mobile clinics to provide quality care at affordable fees for the poor. People are able to avail themselves of treatments for common diseases such as malaria, hernias, baby fevers, baby diarrhea, tuberculosis, and cholera. We offer free HIV testing and dental services and invite medical teams to come from abroad to enhance our medical outreach services.

ORPHANAGES & FAMILIES

GIRLS' HOME: A beautiful home for as many as 50 girls, all of whom have been orphaned or abandoned. This home is sponsored by Grace International.

BOYS' HOME: Boys have their own home. Most of these boys have lost their birth parents in the early stages of their lives. They are taught essential life skills in order to become strong men and leaders in society. Sponsored by Family Christian Residential Services, Pennsylvania USA.

ELDERLY WIDOW'S HOME: A home for the many women whose spouses have passed away, leaving them with no one to turn to. These widows are part of our Grace family, and they keep themselves busy assisting with the care of our boys and girls.

CHILD & FAMILY SPONSORSHIP PROGRAM

While still living at home, children can be sponsored through Grace International. This program is established for children whose parents are still alive but cannot care for them. Through this program you can sponsor a child for education, food, and healthcare. You can also sponsor an entire family.

CHILDREN'S CHRISTMAS PARTY

With the gracious assistance and generous funding of our many friends and partners, Grace International holds an annual Christmas event, for children, staged in numerous locations. The attending boys and girls receive nourishing hot meals and are entertained with music as well as a puppet show dramatic depiction of the story of Christmas. They are afforded salvation opportunities and are blessed with toys and other gifts that they are too poor to, otherwise enjoy.

FEEDING PROGRAM

Hungry children and adults (as funds are available) are fed daily at our Feeding Centers and Schools. This program has brought, and sustained, hope for many, haunted by hunger, thanks to the various groups and individuals who support the program.

SPORTS

To provide some of our youth with a safe and positive environment, a Soccer/Football team was founded in the Bois Caiman area. That team, the B.C.F.J. has excelled in their league and won many championships.

EDUCATION & ECONOMY EMPOWERMENT TRADE SCHOOL:

A vocational/technical school in Thiotte teaches the locals the basic skills for survival and equips them with the tools to improve their quality of life. We are creating a model for trade schools and vocational education to empower the nation with economic stability.

COLLEGE SPONSORSHIP

This program selects the brightest and most ambitious students and funds their way on to higher education, preparing and equipping them to progressively change society and positively transform the nation.

CONFERENCES

Some of the major tools we employ in this great revolution of hope are stadium conferences and leadership training seminars for people from all across Haiti.

MEDIA

Bishop Jeune and his wife Pastor Doris Jeune host their own show on television, broadcast twice a week; it reaches more than 3 million viewers. We also have a radio station located at the Southeast border of Haiti and the Dominican Republic.

Bishop Jeune meets with the media to offer guidance and direction for the nation's people.

ECONOMIC REVOLUTION

Another of our goals is to motivate and educate the Haitian people in successful strategies for their personal and collective entrepreneurship and business ventures. Toward this end we look to develop a community micro-financing system.

ENVIRONMENTAL RESTORATION

Another area of work that we are involved in is Environmental Restoration through reforestation (establishing fruit bearing trees) especially on denuded and flood runoff prone slopes, where crop planting is impractical.

To save trees from harvesting for charcoal production, we are introducing an alternate way of cooking. Burning charcoal as a cooking fuel emits toxic fumes which, when breathed, lead to serious health problems, often with fatal consequences. We are introducing Ethanol/Alcohol Cook stoves in Partnership with GAIA. These stainless steel cook stoves in single and double burner models have been successfully introduced and used, in several African countries, for a number of years.

We will create an agricultural industry growing various crops, such as sweet sorghum, for food and fodder usage and Ethanol production. This will provide agricultural jobs for Haitians as well as better health for both humans and the ecology of the land.

The distillation and distribution of Ethanol will create more jobs thus helping to restore the environment and positively empower the people. Eventually we may be able to retrofit community vehicles to run on Ethanol. Ethanol costs a small fraction of the current and undoubtedly the future price of both charcoal and petrol based gasoline.

FINANCIALLY ACCOUNTABLE

Grace International is accredited nationally by the Evangelical Council for Financial Accountability (ECFA); based on our financial accountability, transparency, sound board governance and ethical fundraising. All donations to Grace International are tax exempt.

SPIRITUAL PURSUITS

International Pastors and Dignitaries celebrating Dedication of Grace Haiti Pediatric Hospital

CHURCHES: Bishop Jeune has helped start and oversees more than 270 churches all across the country of Haiti. The numbers are growing as we continue to share the love and hope of God with the Haitian people.

NATIONAL PASTOR'S CONFERENCES AND SEMINARS: Regular pastoral training seminars bring pastors and leaders from all areas of the country to share and learn leadership skills that will keep them effective in their respective communities.

BIBLE SCHOOL: A school where believers are being trained and equipped to evangelize and spread the gospel. (Sponsored by Pastor Sharon Dougherty and Victory Christian Center, Tulsa, Oklahoma)

FEMMES FERVENTES: Grace International unites women of all ages, races, and denominations through seminars and conferences to empower and equip them to become strong women of God. It is a branch of End Time Handmaidens and Servants International.

POST EARTHQUAKE DEVELOPMENT

Since January 12th, 2010, both of our compounds in Carrefour have become Refuge Centers for earthquake survivors. Our Lamentin compound has sheltered in excess of 25,000 people, making it the second largest tent-camp in Port Au Prince. We are working to resettle the people living in this camp and create small communities that are models of holistic, sustainable and industrious living.

MY GREATEST VICTORY

My greatest victory happened when we were jailed. It made big news and everyone in Haiti was informed that something significant had happened in Bois-Caiman. The judge's verdict was heard by all, "These men did nothing to deserve being arrested and jailed. They were merely preaching the Gospel; just doing God's work. So we shall release them because there is no valid charge against them."

It was a great victory when the government issued a document permitting everyone to go to Bois-Caiman. It was one of our greatest victories because it was an official declaration; recognizing Christian's rights to reclaim the Voodoo co-opted territories. I praise the Lord that my God overcomes all Voodoo!

I have traveled in many countries, 40 states in America, three provinces in Canada as well as to Europe, Central America, Israel, Korea, the Caribbean Islands, Germany, Africa, and elsewhere; preaching the Gospel and informing people, of all these nations, that God has delivered Haiti from the curse of Voodoo, transforming it into a Christian nation. We thank God for what He has been doing.

I remember my youth in the mountains; watching an airplane fly low above me and ducking because I thought it was a giant bird. I never dreamt of flying in one someday. The Lord has blessed me beyond my wildest dreams.

GREAT SATISFACTION FOR ME

My greatest personal satisfaction is witnessing people receiving Christ and growing up in the knowledge of God; later becoming leaders who train others to lead more souls to Christ.

Another of my joys is seeing how many people have become involved in defeating Voodoo. In 1978, the Voodooists constituted 80 percent of the population. Now, according to statistics, Voodoo worshippers have diminished to 3.11 percent of our country's population. Praise God! To realize I have had some small part in this transformation is very satisfying.

I am glad we didn't leave Haiti, when times were tough, but stayed and endured through those difficult early years. Often, the temptation to leave Haiti was unbearably strong. God used His servants, who didn't even know the details of our challenges, to implore us not to give up and leave.

One time, I made a decision to leave for good but didn't tell anyone of my intentions. While I was visiting at Grace Chapel, Papa Luke called me and very strongly said, "Don't leave Haiti".

I just smiled and told him nothing of my plans. Many years later I shared, with him, what had been going on in my life when he told me not to leave Haiti.

Another time, after one of our great crusade meetings, I was with Brother R.W. Schambach. He looked at me sternly and, with a loud voice, proclaimed, "Joel, do not leave Haiti. If you do God will kill you"! I didn't say a word in reply but knew God was speaking to me through His servant. I believe these spiritual, positive changes are some of the fruits of our suffering.

What we are doing continues bearing fruit. As we keep pressing forward to answer God's call and fulfill his vision, more great changes will happen. More amazing blessings will take place in our land. Our country will be transformed forever more. We look forward to the day when our people are set free from economic and spiritual bondage and our various social problems. I'm not saying it's going to be like heaven, but, as our God inspired faithful efforts prevail, Haiti will be better. The next generation will experience better days than what ours has lived through in Haiti.

God brought to our life and ministry many partners who support us financially, help us physically and advice us wisely. It's a great comfort for me to know that I am not in ministry by myself. God has placed many blessed men and women who have caught the vision and work with me. I appreciate His help and for all who have become a part of this ministry. Good things are happening because of them.

CONCLUSION

You Can Be Victorious!

If you have a promise from God; a vision, a dream, and God tells you that some great thing will become of your life but you see that your promise is hidden in a dead end coffin of reality, heading for the cemetery; know that God can create a miracle for your life today. God will resurrect your dream, your vision and His promise for you. Only believe and hold on to the vision He gave you and what He promised you. Don't let go! Many naysayers, around you, may wish you to go to that cemetery of dreams and be buried with your promise. They may insist that nothing will come of your vision and dreams.

If they are in a hurry to get to that cemetery; let them go. They have their own dreams to bury in that cemetery of lost promises but God will bless you, the believer, with a miracle. Believe Him for that miracle! Believe Him for a Resurrection!

Don't worry about where you came from. Your origins are not that important. What are you doing with God's plan for your life? Do you understand God's plan for your life? Do you accept His plan for your life? No matter how big it is the Lord can make it happen. Others may try to make your decisions for you; trying to decide what you are going to be; to determine your destiny.

Follow God's directions. Be obedient to Him. Let Him lead you through the wilderness, the mountains, valleys and dark times. Follow Him up the glory road towards the beacon of light He's shining to lead you home. God will make of you what some said you would never become. How can they see what is the covenant between you and God? If you have a vision, know that God will lead you to its fruition.

The secret to victory in your life begins by acknowledging that you cannot do everything on your own. We cannot be victorious by ourselves and realize victories on our own. We must recognize and admit our weaknesses and lean on God's strength. By ourselves, we cannot achieve the level that God wants us to attain. We need fellow believers to supportively pray with us that we might attain the goal God wants for us. Lift every obstacle, large or small, up to Him that He may move it out of your way. We must first win the victory in our own lives.

First, you must defeat the little "foxes" in your mind before you can be victorious over the lions in the arena of life. Get God on your side and you cannot lose.

The world around us holds much to distract us from Him. Keep your eyes on the prize; the vision that God has blessed you with. Keep your eyes on the reward because it's waiting for you all along the road of your life.

God will give you the strength to keep on keeping on. The Holy Spirit will always be your comforter and helper. When we are weak, He gives us the strength to go on, until we arrive at the destination God desires for us, with the talents He endowed us with. I encourage you to not give up. Don't be a quitter. Keep swimming till you get to the other side. It takes faith and determination to believe that God will not forsake you in the middle of the stream. Victory awaits you on the other side! **Quitters never win and Winners never quit!**

God has brought me a long way since . . . I sneezed in my casket. You see, **God cannot lie!**

VICTORIOUS SCRIPTURES

Ye have not chosen me, but I have chosen you, and ordained you, that you should go and bring forth fruit, and that your fruit should remain: that whatsoever

ye shall ask of the Father in my name, He may give it to you. John 15:16

9. For we are labourers together with God: ye are God's husbandry, ye are God's building.

10. According to the grace of God which is given unto me, as a wise masterbuilder, I have laid the foundation, and another buildeth thereon. But let every man take heed how he buildeth thereupon.

11. For other foundation can no man lay than that is laid, which is Jesus-Christ.

12. Now if a man build upon this foundation gold, silver, precious stones, wood, hay, stubble;

13. Every man's work shall be made manifest: for the day shall declare it, because it shall be revealed by fire; and the fire shall try every man's work of what sort it is.

14. If any man's work abide which he hath built thereupon, he shall receive a reward. I Corinthians 3:9-14

EPILOGUE

I met Bishop Joel at Christian Retreat in Florida on His first trip to Florida. After Joel and his wife Doris got married, God supernaturally connected us together.

On my trip the following year to Haiti, the group I took down with me, were able to see the work, that they started, first hand. God tugged on our hearts when we saw the need to feed the children who were coming to school. So we started a feeding program back in the early seventy's which is still going on today.

During a season of trials when Bishop Joel was considering to leave Haiti, I told him that I felt that he could serve God the best ministering to his own people and staying in Haiti. After 12 years he shared with me that it was my encouragement that kept him in Haiti.

It was after this that the work began to grow. Today after being involved with Bishop Joel for over 40 years, I do recognize a true Apostolic Anointing and a man of integrity who has become a Mighty leader for Haiti.

Bishop Joel is one of my sons in the faith and he and his wife Doris are a part of our Family.

Dr. Luke Weaver, Sr.
Founder of Grace Chapel Mission
Elizabethtown, Pennsylvania

AFTERWORD

My association with my visionary friends Bishop Joel and Pastor Doris Jeune began shortly after Hurricane Allen devastated Haiti in 1980. A deadly drought followed with rampant death by starvation. Because orphaned boys were deemed of more value, the tiny girls remained vulnerable to the extreme. Pastor Joel took a load of food to the mountains and brought home a load of orphaned girls to go with some they had already taken in.

Some farmers from central Kansas heard of the plight and immediately began helping the Jeunes' with their girls and with their extensive visions for the newly purchased land. Now, 31 years later, most of the visions have been realized.

That the multiple ministries that have contributed to these accomplishments are of God; and the work done under the auspices of the Holy Spirit; and for the Love of Jesus the Christ, is apparent to all who witness these great works.

Salvation under the Jeunes is spiritual, physical, moral, academic and economic . . . and the old devil doesn't like it!

Our prayer is for great success in all the ministries and this book beginning with the miraculous sneeze.

James T. "Ted" Grimes, M.D. Rtd.
Chairman, Haiti Love & Faith Ministries, Inc.
Partners with Star of Hope International of America

WORDS OF RECOMMENDATION

I was honored and humbled when asked by Bishop Jeune to write something about his book for a few reasons. First of all, he has an amazing story that should not be overlooked and cannot be ignored. Secondly, I have been allowed the opportunity to see him and his wife Doris at work and in their home, in good times and not so good times, at serious moments and in times of laughter and I've seen them focus their passion, conviction, and commitment to the things that they stand for. They are true servants and true leaders.

Meron Abraha
Philadelphia Based Artist and Businessman

Bishop Joel Jeune is a man on a mission. In the forty years I have known him, observed him, preached on platforms by his side and watched him build and lead his successful ministry enterprise, I've never seen him waver from the call of God upon his life to evangelize his homeland, Haiti. Despite his popularity and extraordinary opportunities, he has stayed humble and committed, choosing the pulpit over politics and people over possessions. Joel Jeune is touchable, likeable, always positive and enthusiastic. Together, with his wife Doris, they are revered as spiritual parents and mentors by the younger generations and admired by trusted leaders throughout the world. Joel Jeune's story is a testimony of God's Divine providence and provision. It is an encouragement to every believer to stay the course keep the faith and simply trust God.

Doctor Phil Derstine
Gospel Crusade, Inc. President
Christian Retreat, Senior Pastor

I have known and had the privilege of working with Bishop Joel Jeune for many years. I have found him to be a man of tremendous faith and a steadfast champion of the Haitian people. The call of God on his life is so unmistakably strong that he has at times become a target of political figures in Haiti that would like to silence him. Yet he transcends politics and remains true to his apostolic vision for his country.

This amazing story, beginning with a miraculous resurrection, will explain why he must continue where others would have given up long ago.

Rev. J. David Gingrich
President, Gospel Crusade of Canada

I met Bishop Joel and Sister Doris through TBN. Being French, I am attracted to all ex-French colonies, naturally and spiritually. The first time I went to Haiti, "The Pearl of the Antilles" (if not in this world, then in the new heaven and new earth), I was astounded by the spiritual evidence of evil.

Bishop Joel and Sister Doris' compound (house, orphanages, churches, etc.) was light and life. The rest of the land was darkness and death. Everything spiritual is more pronounced there and more real making the work stand out; a visible contrast between the Grace of God and the curse the devil brings.

Bishop Joel shows God's desire for the land. He and his strong wife Doris Jeune are in a continual upstream battle, and their faith is helping keep the nation afloat. Perseverance, faithfulness, and hard work with true love, undergird the ministry.

When it was time to take back the land for the Gospels sake, I was privileged to be a part of going up to the high places of Voodoo on the island in order to take them back for the kingdom of God. There I witnessed the power of God. Bishop Joel was arrested and put in jail for three days for his faith; and his resistance to evil and the Voodoo in the government. I saw the high place dry up and die for good; then the spiritual war intensified. Later, Bishop Joel fought to help put Christians in government, a never ending fight. Still, they persist because they know God.

We also went later to New Orleans to continue in the war against that very same Voodoo. Haitians roots found their way there. The backlash is incredible. I can say that through it all, Bishop Joel Jeune and Sister Doris Jeune have persisted and continue today in feeding thousands of orphans and hungry children, are raising hundreds of orphanages, are establishing schools and clinics, and are preaching the word and love of God through the land.

Their grace is a continual rain refreshing their people. Every one helping is touched by them.

They have shown me and my husband Warren, GOD ON EARTH.

Suzanne Schreier

I have been, for twenty-three years, under the ministry of Bishop Joel and Mrs. Doris Jeune. From the times where they challenged the false teachings of the Roman Catholic Church of Haiti, to the times where the demonic masks of Bois-Caiman fell down and were trampled underfoot before the power of the blood of Jesus, via their struggle against injustice, abuse, poverty and illiteracy; I learned in a practical way what full time ministry is about. It is having your all heart, soul, mind and strength penetrated by a passion for God manifested by a compassion for others. It is accepting to become daily a true and living sacrifice.

In the Haitian context, we would precede dawn to catch the faithful renewal of God's mercy. It would regenerate patience, wisdom, intelligence, discernment, grace, wealth and energy that we need to face the challenges that would flow over us till sunset. When came the time to sleep, on our bed, we would review the movie of the day in our mind. We weep for our incapacity to treat the sufferings of our people, we ask God to forgive our failures, we praise Him for the accomplishments and rejoice in Him for making our live a blessing to others.

Living by the sides of the Jeune's is preparing yourself to be sensitive to the goodness of God minute after minute, to keep a record of His miracles day after day, to write a book year after year. I am glad that Reverend and Mrs. Jeune have finally decided to pass on to the next generation some part of what God had been doing in them, with them and around them.

After reading the manuscript of these existing testimonies, I have made of Caleb's request to Joshua my prayer: "Lord, give me this mountain." May the life, the ministry of the Jeune family shared in **I SNEEZED IN MY CASKET** urge you to go further in your journey with our wonderful Savior: the Lord Jesus Christ. Thanks for the honor of being part of your ministry.

Bishop Eddy Saintange Volcy
Senior Pastor of Christian Church of Grace
Montreal, Quebec, Canada

I have personally known Doris Jeune since 1968 when we were both 14 years old and my folks took our family to Haiti for the first time. I watched as she married and worked along-side Pastor Joel and saw their ministry grow from just one church, and no children, to having four of their own and all these many that call them mommy and poppy, and the churches and ministries that extend from God, through them to bless many in Haiti and around the world.

Along with my wife Bonnie and the church here in New Brunswick, Canada, we are honored to work with such a fine couple and know that Gods favor is overtaking them and flowing over to the multitudes they minister to and touch.

Pastors Luke Jr. and Bonnie Weaver
Village Lighthouse
Benton, New Brunswick, Canada

I have known Bishop Joel and Doris Jeune for over 40 years. When My Father Luke Weaver would go over to Haiti, I would go along with him. I was always challenged by seeing how little he had and how much they were doing for their people. I have been blessed to be a part of their lives and ministries down through the years. When God puts you together there are no circumstances or people who can separate you. We are truly brothers and sisters in Christ.

I have seen God use Bishop Joel and Doris Jeune like He did Daniel of old who was taken as a slave and because he knew his God and who he was in the hands of God and always was a man of integrity became a savior of the known world.

God is using them to transform Haiti into a country that will be given back to God. Bishop Joel is raising up a new breed of Haitians to take the country from the devil and give it back to Gods people.

You will truly be blessed as you read the story of how God is using them to transform Haiti today.

Pastor Melvin Weaver
Senior Pastor of Grace Chapel Missions
Elizabethtown, Pennsylvania

I have known Bishop Joel for several years, been with Him in Haiti and seen the work he and his wife Doris are doing for the Kingdom. It is very evident that God has a plan for Joel's life and raised him from the dead to accomplish His will. Every time I visit with Joel I find out something else he is involved in. I think we will only know in eternity all he has done for the Lord. Because of his humble heart I think most people will never know the impact his life is having on the people of Haiti.

Rev. David White, Pastor
Word of Life Christian Center
Bartow, Florida

GOD'S PLAN FOR YOUR VICTORY!

"What must I do to be saved?" is the cry of men and women; God's Word, the Bible, provides clear answers.

ACKNOWLEDGE YOUR SIN

And the publican, standing afar off, would not lift up so much as his eyes unto heaven, but smote upon his breast, saying, God be merciful to me a sinner. —Luke 18:13

For all have sinned, and come short of the glory of God. —Romans 3:23

REPENT OF YOUR SIN

Repent ye therefore, and be converted, that your sins may be blotted out, when the times of refreshing shall come from the presence of the Lord. —Acts 3:19

". . . except' ye repent, ye shall all likewise perish." —Luke 13:3

CONFESS YOUR SIN

That if thou shalt confess with thy mouth the Lord Jesus, and shalt believe in thine heart that God hath raised him from the dead, thou shalt be saved. —Romans 10:9

If we confess our sins, he is faithful and just to forgive us our sins, and to cleanse us from all unrighteousness. —1 John 1:9

FORSAKE THE PAST

Let the wicked forsake his way, and the unrighteous man his thoughts: and let him return unto the LORD, and he will have mercy upon him; and to our God, for he will abundantly pardon.
—Isaiah 55:7

BELIEVE IN THE LORD

For God so loved the world, that he gave his only begotten Son, that whosoever believeth in him should not perish, but have everlasting life.
—John 3:16

He that believeth and is baptized shall be saved; but he that believeth not shall be damned.
—Mark 16:16

RECEIVE THE GIFT OF ETERNAL LIFE

He came unto his own, and his own received him not. But as many as received him, to them gave He power to become the sons of God, even to them that believe on His name. —John 1:11-12

If you have not made your eternal decision, you can make it right now! It is so profound, so eternal, yet in many cases, so simple. Pray the following words now:

"Lord Jesus, I believe You died for my sins and I ask Your forgiveness. I ask you to come into my heart. I receive You now as my personal Savior and invite You to control my life from this day forward. Amen!"

God wants to give you a new life of peace and victory. God wants to give you the peace that passes all human understanding. By faith, receive what God has already done for you!

Thank you for reading about all that God has done for me. To Him be all the glory! You might not have been raised up from a casket at a funeral procession, like I was, but you do have some degree of God's call on your life.

I want to personally invite you to visit Haiti and witness our work. There are numerous opportunities for medical teams, short term missions, ministry and work teams to help our children, widows or other worthy projects.

Please partner with us to nourish the children and families that would, without our help, go hungry and be neglected. We would be so grateful and honored if God would lead you to make a tax-deductible contribution investment. Anyone wishing to send donations please make checks payable to Grace International and send them to the address below. We can also accept donations on line at www.graceintl.org.

God is impacting the nation of Haiti in an unprecedented way.

If this book has been a genuine blessing to you and you would like further information; if you believed the scriptures and prayed the prayer on the previous pages and you would like to contact me, please write:

Joel R. Jeune, D.D.

Grace International, Inc.
P.O. Box 172508
Hialeah, FL 33017

Phone: 305-231-1117
Fax: 305-231-1118

"http://www.graceintl.org"
E-mail: graceoffice7@yahoo.com

The Spirit of the Lord is on me, because he has anointed me to preach good news to the poor. He has sent me to proclaim freedom for the prisoners and recovery of sight for the blind, to release the oppressed. —Luke 4:18 (NIV)

Dr. Bishop Joel R Jeune

INDEX

C

D

E

F

G

H

I

J

K

L

M

N

O

T

U

V

W

Y

CPSIA information can be obtained at www.ICGtesting.com
Printed in the USA
LVOW041223071212

310173LV00003BA/7/P